Driving Mr. Albert

Michael Paterniti

"Wildly offbeat—a professor-and-the-madman tale with a little coming-of-age and an image of Tupperware that you'll never forget."
—*Vogue*

"A quirky and engaging book . . . Readers will tag along on this trip to a surprising ending."—*USA Today*

"Huge appeal and final joy . . . Paterniti recalls the all-embracing ecumenism of Twain's *Roughing It* or *Life on the Mississippi*."
—*The Washington Post*

"Part travelogue, part biography . . . highly absorbing."—*Vanity Fair*

"The road trip is hilariously deconstructed."—*Harper's Bazaar*

"It's impossible to put the book down. Paterniti has written a work at once entertaining, psychologically rich and emotionally sophisticated—a feat as rare as, well, Einstein himself."
—*Publishers Weekly,* starred review

"Alternately hilarious, moving, and always insightful."
—*The Austin Chronicle*

"A cerebral adventure . . . wonderful . . . whimsical, surreal."
—*Men's Journal*

"Gorgeous prose . . . [An] unforgettable trip."—*The Denver Post*

Please turn the page for more extraordinary acclaim. . . .

"We all need to sign up for this one, the last great postmodern, *fin de millennium* roadtrip, a cosmic who-dun-it and an everlastingly unforgettable pilgrimage. *Driving Mr. Albert* is a dazzling dense lump of miracles and genius thanks in no small part to chief detective Michael Paterniti, a literary wizard whose multi-dimensional prose is quite a match for his subject's brilliance."
—Bob Shacochis, author of
Easy in the Islands and *The Immaculate Invasion*

"A fun, diverting ride . . . In prose that leaps from operatically lyrical to absurdly comical, Paterniti combines brilliant sketches of encounter on the road with innocent musings and choice historical trivia."—*US Weekly*

"Paterniti's book reaches beyond the madcap adventures of their cross-country trip . . . to deliver an extraordinary portrait of Harvey, of Paterniti himself, and of the nation that embraces them both."
—*Esquire*

"[A] most unusual book—part cross-country travelogue, part sideshow, part Einstein biography, part profile of a unique character named Thomas Harvey . . ."—*The Dallas Morning News*

"Paterniti's unique and haunting tale illuminates our dream of immortality and life's ever-confounding blend of the prosaic and the miraculous."—*Booklist,* starred review

"*Driving Mr. Albert* is lyrical and comical, witty and bitter, and dazzling at times. The most unusual of subjects is presented in clear, heartfelt prose that made this reader glad he was along for the ride."—*BookPage*

"Entertaining . . . Paterniti does an excellent job."
—*San Francisco Chronicle*

Driving Mr. Albert

——

A Trip Across America
with Einstein's Brain

M ICHAEL P ATERNITI

A DIAL PRESS TRADE PAPERBACK

DRIVING MR. ALBERT
A Dial Press Trade Paperback Book

PUBLISHING HISTORY
Dial Press hardcover edition / 2000
Delta Trade Paperback edition / June 2001
Dial Press Trade Paperback edition / July 2005

Published by
Bantam Dell
A Division of Random House, Inc.
New York, New York

ISBN: 978-0-385-33303-0

Reprinted by arrangement with The Dial Press

Published simultaneously in Canada

For Sara and Leo,
all the days and nights of us yet to come

And in memory of Peggy Fulton Corbett

It was a splendid mind. For if thought is like the keyboard of a piano, divided into so many notes, or like the alphabet is ranged in twenty-six letters all in order, then his mind had no difficulty in running over those letters one by one, firmly, accurately, until it had reached, say, the letter Q. He reached Q. . . . But after Q? What comes next? After Q there are a number of letters the last of which is scarcely visible to mortal eyes, but glimmers red in the distance. . . . How many men in a thousand million, he asked himself, reach Z after all? Surely the leader of a forlorn hope may ask himself that, and answer, without treachery to the expedition behind him, "One perhaps." One in a generation.

—Virginia Woolf, *To the Lighthouse*

Prologue ◆ The White Rabbit

To be honest I thought the road trip would be a caper. That's what I imagined. And I thought the old doctor was a true eccentric, which would be entertaining. And yet desire is a tricky thing. It can change a quick outing to the store for milk into a lifelong, shoeless quest through the Himalayas in search of enlightenment. It can put you on the road to Canterbury without your realizing it at first. And some version of that is what happened.

I first heard the story of Albert Einstein's brain as an urban myth too weird to believe. A friend had a friend who'd heard about it from someone else living in Roswell or Sedona or somewhere like that, a bit of geographical detail that was meant to lend either credibility or incredibility to the yarn, I couldn't tell which. My friend told me about it during a commercial break while we were watching the Gulf War, which would have made me about twenty-five years old at the time. And somehow, the war and the brain conflated in my mind. Even now, when I imagine Einstein's dendrites and neurons firing as his brain lit upon relativity, I picture Baghdad, with its minarets and modern-antennaed buildings sparkling beneath thousands of phantasmagorical tracers, under Allied attack on a very dark night.

The tale went like this: Einstein died in 1955 and, during an autopsy, his brain was removed from his head, ostensibly to be studied for the keys to its genius. But then, after some years, the brain supposedly disappeared. Rumor had it that it had been cut up and parts of it resided somewhere in a garage in Saskatchewan, next to the basketballs and hockey sticks of some oil rigger's kids, collecting dust. Other parts were said to belong to the doctor who did the autopsy, an odd man who had since vanished.

I loved that, the Canadian stash, the weird immortality of the brain, its allegedly bizarre keeper. As time passed, I began to repeat the story of Einstein's brain to friends and acquaintances adding my own flourishes. The old doctor with Einstein's brain now occasionally wore an eye patch or was a hunchback. Sometimes, he was pursued by secret agents or ex-lovers with an ax to grind, which kept him moving from town to town. In other versions, he was looking to sell the brain on the black market. Only later would I find out how close I'd been to certain kernels of the truth.

As time passed, I thought less and less frequently about Einstein's brain, filed it in life's arcana file. But several years later, living in New Mexico, I struck up a friendship with my landlord, a man named Steven, who randomly happened to be friends with the writer William Burroughs. A veteran of all things cool and outré, Steven often watered the flower garden in his adobe compound where I lived. When I told him about Einstein's brain, he didn't even blink. "Yeah, the guy with the brain lives next to William in Lawrence, Kansas," he said.

I thought he was putting me on. "He what?" I said.

"Yeah," he said. "He used to be a pathologist." Then he kept spraying his snowdrops and daffodils with the hose, unfazed.

"Like . . ."

". . . lives next door?" Steven said, completing my sentence. He looked at me sideways with the slightest trace of pity. "Yeah, the doc's a real trippy dude, but they've hung out."

"Trippy dude?"

"Weird cat."

Oh, trippy dude *and* weird cat. How weird? Weird in what way? Like Norman Bates or Boris Karloff weird, with a basement full of smoking potions and beakers of fluorescent liquid and some strange Frankenstein cloning experiment in progress? Like August Strindberg, in dementia, trying to turn lead to gold? Or weird as in culturally accepted, iconoclastically weird, a cult figure like, say, Burroughs himself, or a shaggy Indian mystic like Rabindranath Tagore?

"I don't know," said Steven, but then he offered to get the old doctor's number for me, from Burroughs himself. Which he did, delivered on a slip of paper torn from a notebook. And I immediately pinned it to the bulletin board near my desk at work, stared at it for a month, then just started dialing. As I went through my days working as a magazine editor, I'd look at that number and, for no justifiable reason, I'd pick up the phone and dial. The line rang but no one answered and there was no answering machine.

After four months—who was weird now?—I vowed to myself that I'd quit dialing. But I couldn't. I varied the hours of calling; I tried once at midnight just to see. Finally, I gave myself three more chances. On the first one, someone picked up.

"Hello." He said it like "halo."

"Uhhh . . . Is this Thomas Harvey?"

"Way-ell, yes, it sure is." The man sounded friendly.

"Okay, right . . . ," I stumbled, "where to begin. I'm . . . I'm . . ." Blood rushed to my head and I could hear my own voice, tinny and unsure. Who was I? And what did I really want from him? I stammered again. Then, I asked if he was the man with Einstein's brain, and when he confirmed that he was, I remember moving my lips but not speaking: *Holy shit!* Emboldened, I wondered aloud about the possibility of meeting him someday. He vaguely agreed that, yes, it'd be nice to meet someday. But even as we spoke, he must have known that he was leaving Kansas, packing his worldly possessions in one car, as he'd done almost forty years earlier when he quietly fled Princeton, New Jersey, after the accusations that his removal of Einstein's brain was really an act of theft. And the next thing I knew,

Dr. Harvey simply disappeared on me. A disconnected line, no for-warding address. Like Alice's White Rabbit—vanished.

During the ensuing months, I quit my job and, along with my girl-friend, Sara, moved back East, to Maine. And all the while, I couldn't shake the thought of Harvey and Einstein's brain, like a fortune cookie promising something so oddly enticing that you can't let go. So, I began again. I tried to track Harvey's family members, which proved difficult. I called another doctor, Sandra Witelson in Hamilton, Canada, with whom Harvey was supposedly working. Much to my surprise, Witelson seemed to know all about me. "Dr. Harvey has said all he wants to say to you," she said with such unex-pected surliness that I was sure he hadn't. She claimed not to know where he was, but then at the same time she said she wouldn't give me his new number. Another six months passed, and by sheer per-sistence I found the number. On my first try, Harvey picked up the phone in what I would later learn was a 1950s ranch house near Princeton, New Jersey, where he was living now with his sixty-seven-year-old girlfriend.

"Way-ell, it sure is good to hear from you," he said, and he seemed to mean it. We talked. He agreed to meet. On a weekday just after Thanksgiving, I drove south from Maine through dead leaves and chimney smoke, past trees that appeared in a chill autumn mist like candelabra. Dr. Harvey greeted me at the door in a red-and-white plaid shirt and a thin, solid-blue Pendleton tie that still bore a mildewy $10 price tag from some earlier decade. His face was blowsy and peckled, runneled with lines, though he didn't quite seem his eighty-four years. He had an eagle nose, alert eyes, and stubbed yel-low teeth. His white hair was as fine as corn silk and shifted with the November wind over the bald patches on his head. He had no eye patch or hunchback—only a slight limp from a bicycling accident he had suffered a few years earlier. He told me he'd been hit by a car driven by a "female octogenarian" while riding to work, and now one leg was slightly shorter than the other. I couldn't help but wonder what eighty-four-year-old works, let alone rides his bike to work?

He led me to a dank basement where he'd set up a makeshift office strewn with scientific journals. On a table sat a microscope covered by a small plastic tarp. He stoked a fire and offered me a seat on a lime-green chintz couch among crocheted rugs and genie bottles of blown glass, Ethiopian cookbooks and macramé. He didn't impress me right away as a rebel or a Casanova or a Beat wanderer, as a hero or a thief or a holy man—all of which, in various moments, he later would. But there were still little things that gave him away. A green beret hung on a hook. Books occupied shelves with titles like: *How to Make Love to the Same Person for the Rest of Your Life, Romantic Jealousy,* and *Open Marriage.* And then, how did a man with a Yale education and Einstein's brain in his possession come to live in such reduced circumstances, holding court in the basement of his girlfriend's house?

The doctor seemed to take it all as a matter of course. He brought tea, and we sat for a while, two men from different corners of a century, camped near a warm fire, stirring sugar into our Lipton before the future arrived. Before everybody upped and moved to lunar colonies, I was finally sitting with Dr. Thomas Harvey, like some groupie pilgrim, waiting for him to speak.

Part One

1 ◆ The Devil Craps on the Big Pile

Albert Einstein was born in 1879, in Ulm, Germany, with a head shaped like a lopsided medicine ball. Beholding it for the first time, his grandmother fell into complete shock. "Much too fat!" she exclaimed. "Much too fat!" His mother was also horrified, believing she'd delivered a monster. The boy didn't speak until he was three; even then he would move his lips for a long time before anything came out. Everyone figured that he was *zurückgeblieben*, retarded.

By his own recollections, young Albert lived mostly in his mind, built intricate card houses, and marveled at a compass his father showed him as a boy. Kids in his neighborhood called him The Bore because he refused to roughhouse, and only when he couldn't avoid them would he offer himself as an umpire in their games. For the most part he was a loner, preferring the company of his uncles because they could explain the family business to him: electricity. As it was, he believed much less in people than in the things of the world. When his sister, Maja, was born, young Albert stared down into the bassinet, crestfallen, and according to family members said, "Yes, but where are its wheels?"

In school, contrary to legend, he received mostly good grades. Still, he chafed at the authoritarian regimentation of the German education system and showed his sly sense of humor early on, mocking his teachers to the laughter of classmates. He was dazzled by his first geometry book, by the symmetries and angles of the universe, and transfixed by the generators that were manufactured in his father's factory. While his parents had grand ambitions for their only son— they were part of a first generation of Jews allowed to own property and pursue higher education in Germany—Albert himself undertook his own plan of self-education. By the age of ten, he was reading Euclid and devouring the science books of his day. He also fell under a spell of deep religiosity during which he refused to eat pork and composed hymns to God, which he chanted as he walked the streets. But according to Einstein, he abandoned the Jewish faith at the age of twelve, when his science training revealed to him that "much in the stories of the Bible could not be true."

If most of his instructors underestimated him—a Greek teacher once told him he wouldn't amount to anything in life—Albert Einstein had a certain confidence, what his elders came to see as supercilious arrogance. The problem was that their upstart student didn't hesitate to point out their intellectual shortcomings or call out their hypocrisy, which became all the more rankling because he was so often right. He voraciously devoured what stood between him and originality—namely mediocrity—and they mistook this drive for impudence. "You are a smart boy, Einstein, a very smart boy," his university physics professor told him. "But you have one great fault: You'll never let yourself be told anything." Einstein's general response, written to a friend sometime later, was curt and impassioned: "Unthinking respect for authority is the greatest enemy of truth."

As a teenager he moved from Munich to Italy to Switzerland, renouncing his German citizenship to avoid military service, which marked the beginning of his pacifism. As a man, he grew into a powerful body with thick arms and legs and raffish good looks: an ironic, mischievous smile, a full head of dark, curly hair, and a soft, dreamy gaze. He was flatfooted, about five-feet-six, and liked to hike and sail. He played the violin—Mozart, Bach, Schubert. And though not a great violinist, his music-making was an essential part of his life.

After injuring his hand as a university student, he wrote to his duet partner, a woman, claiming he greatly missed "his old friend"—the violin "through whom I say & sing to myself everything that, in sober thoughts, I often do not even admit to myself, or at most laugh at when I see in others."

In his approach to his work, Einstein's childhood led seamlessly to his adulthood, when he spent most of his days sitting still, dreaming of the universe, pondering the weight of the moon or the orbit of Mercury. In 1905, toiling as a twenty-six-year-old patent clerk (he couldn't find a teaching job because none of his former teachers would recommend him) in Bern, Switzerland, he conceived the special theory of relativity and the equation $E=mc^2$, a supposition that all matter, from a feather to a rock, contains energy.

During that one year in the Patent Office—what's known as Einstein's *annus mirabilis*—he scribbled five groundbreaking papers, all published in the prestigious German journal *Annalen der Physik,* catapulting him from complete obscurity to fame. The impact of that year is still confounding today, for nearly a century later, we're dealing with the aftermath of a universe predicated on the Einsteinian observation that among other things, the flow of time is relative for each person. When the first flicker of relativity occurred to him after months of puzzling with his close friend Michele Besso, he turned to the man and said, "Thank you. I've completely solved the problem."

Recognizing a revolution in their midst, the leading scientists of Einstein's day soon came to visit him on the top floor at the Patent Office, and shortly thereafter he received a progression of teaching appointments in Bern, Zurich, Prague, and finally Munich. With his theories that predicted the origin, nature, and destiny of the universe, Einstein toppled Newton and nearly three hundred years of science. The greatest scientific achievements of our century—electronics, the atomic bomb, space travel—were all suggested in those 1905 pages and then refined in decades to come.

What followed, too, was the general theory of relativity, which Einstein formulated in March of 1916. The theory was confirmed during a solar eclipse three years later by Arthur Eddington, an English astronomer who observed that starlight actually swerved as it passed the sun, to the exact degree predicted by Einstein, proving that light has mass and that there are curvatures in space-time caused by gravity, which, among other things, explained how and why the earth was held in orbit around the sun. In an instant, Albert Einstein was world-famous. His mysterious smile beamed from the front pages of newspapers around the world—a genius, a guru-mystic who had unlocked the secrets of God's own mind.

Inundated with invitations from Hollywood to Lahore, Einstein embarked on a world tour. He was feted by kings and emperors, presidents and movie stars, tweedling into the world's most hallowed halls in a bemused state of sockless dishevelment. Hopelessly absentminded, he left his luggage on train platforms, used uncashed checks as bookmarks. He claimed he got his hairstyle—eventually a wild, electric-white nimbus—"through negligence." Explaining his overall sloppiness, he said, "It would be a sad situation if the wrapper were better than the meat wrapped inside it." He laughed like a barking seal, snored like a foghorn, sunbathed in the nude. And then took tea with the queen.

Everywhere, it was Einstein mania. He went to Shanghai, Tokyo, Jerusalem, Rio. Arriving for the first time in Manhattan in 1921 aboard the SS *Rotterdam*, Einstein wandered down the gangplank to clamoring throngs with his violin case tucked under his arm, looking more like a concert musician than a scientist. *The New York Times* urged its readers not to be offended by the fact that only twelve people in the world truly understood the work of "the suddenly famous Dr. Einstein." In London, he was asked to explain his theory at the Palladium for three weeks on the same bill as fire-eaters and tightrope walkers at whatever fee. "At the Chrysanthemum Festival," wrote one German diplomat stationed in Japan, "it was neither the empress nor the prince regent nor the imperial princes who held reception; everything turned around Einstein."

In the years to follow, Einstein's fame would only grow. He vehemently criticized the Nazis and became a target for German ultranationalists, who waited outside his home, hurling anti-Semitic obscenities at him. In 1933, a German newspaper reported that *Fehme*, an extreme nationalist organization, had put a bounty of five thousand dollars on Einstein's head. When he heard the news, Einstein touched his hair and said, "I did not know it was worth so much." Then he fled, first to Britain, and on to the United States—to Princeton—where, in 1940, he became an American citizen.

Meanwhile, he received honorary degrees from Oxford, Cambridge, the Sorbonne, Harvard, and scores of other universities around the world. With each new award or trophy—none of which seemed to matter a whit to the scientist—he uttered in German, "The devil craps on the big pile." A copy of the special theory of relativity in Einstein's scrawl was auctioned off in 1944 for $6 million. And yet, by the time Einstein moved to America, his work had become much less influential in scientific circles, where the emphasis was now on quantum mechanics, a theory that described a highly volatile and unpredictable reality at the molecular level, something Einstein could not bring himself to accept. "God does not play dice with the universe," he said in one of his most famously quoted statements.

Instead, he spent the last two decades of his life diligently working at Princeton's Institute for Advanced Study on his own unified field theory, one that attempted to balance ideas about gravity and electromagnetism in hopes of forming a more complete understanding of the universe. Though he worked in vain, this period was memorable for his high-profile pacifism and moral outrage at a world gone awry. For some, his political proclamations were as important as Gandhi's, and because he, too, became regarded as a kind of prophet, David Ben-Gurion, prime minister of the nascent Israeli state, felt compelled to offer Einstein the presidency of his country in 1952. To the relief of Ben-Gurion and most others in the fledgling Israeli government, he declined.

In the last lonely years of his life, Einstein was struck with frequent attacks of nausea that culminated in diarrhea or vomiting. An exam revealed an aneurysm in his abdominal aorta, but Einstein refused an operation and anticipated his own demise. "I want to be cremated so people won't come to worship at my bones," he said.

On the night before he died, April 17, 1955, lying in bed at Princeton Hospital, the seventy-six-year-old Einstein asked to see his most recent pages of calculations, typically working until the end. Sometime earlier he had told a friend, "I have finished my task here." And a few weeks before, after the death of his dear lifelong friend Michele Besso, who had acted as such an able sounding board for his theory of relativity, he had written, "Now he has preceded me a little by parting from this strange world. This means nothing. To us believing physicists the distinction between past, present, and future has only the significance of a stubborn illusion."

The next morning, April 18, the chief pathologist of the hospital arrived: Dr. Thomas Stoltz Harvey, then a strapping forty-two-year-old with Montgomery Clift good looks, a wife and two boys at home, and a bright future ahead. He went to his office in the bowels of the hospital, then followed the water pipes along the ceiling of a dark hallway to the morgue where Einstein's body was laid out, naked and mottled, on a gurney.

"Imagine my surprise," Harvey said to me that afternoon in the basement of his girlfriend's house, embers from the fire bottle-rocketing into a metal screen, then falling to the stone below. "A fellow up in New York, my former teacher Dr. Harry Zimmerman"—and an acquaintance of Einstein's—"was going to do the autopsy. But then he couldn't get away. He rang me up, and we agreed that I'd do it." Harvey then trotted out his credentials for me: He had worked under Zimmerman, who was a neuroanatomist, at Yale and had also taught two years of neuroanatomy for Dr. Fritz Lewy at the University of Pennsylvania. He explained that Lewy had been the head of the Neurological Institute in Berlin before Hitler, and that he was world-famous for having "discovered some inclusion bodies in the brain cells in Alzheimer's disease, which are now known as Lewy bodies." He held forth on Lewy for a while, perhaps by way of conferring some of Lewy's résumé on himself.

Harvey, by contrast, grew up in a Kentucky line of dyed-in-the-wool Quakers, spent an uneventful childhood in Louisville, then moved to Hartford, Connecticut, when his father got a good job with an insurance firm. Later, he attended Yale, both as an undergraduate and as a medical student. In his third year of med school, he contracted tuberculosis and spent the next year in a sanatorium—a dark time during which he was confined to a bed and rocking chair and, according to Harvey, saw several friends die around him. When he emerged in the real world again, he turned to pathology because "the hours were less demanding." That year of sickness, he would tell me later, was one of the greatest disappointments of his life.

And April 18, 1955, was one of his greatest triumphs. The world press descended on Princeton; the Einstein family was ensconced at 112 Mercer Street, the place where the great scientist had lived out his final days. And yet when Harvey describes his conversation with Zimmerman regarding who would perform the autopsy, the whole thing sounds like two friends trying to work out arrangements for dropping off a broken car at the garage. That Monday morning, at approximately eight, Harvey pushed open the morgue door on a cramped, brightly lit, green-tiled room full of vacuums, water hoses, silver bowls, a refrigerator where bodies were kept in large metal trays, and a scale with the brand name Chatillon, to measure the weight of the newly excised organs. He says that he felt awe when he came face-to-face with the world-famous physicist, lying alone in the pale light.

Harvey says he took a scalpel in his fingers and sliced Albert Einstein open with a Y incision, tracing down from each collarbone and scoring the belly, the skin giving like cellophane. Like hundreds of other autopsies he'd performed, he exposed the marbled meat of the ribs and a layer of mustard-yellow fat. He pulled back two heavy flaps of skin, like drapes, took a saw in his right hand, and cut open Einstein's chest. Inside, the wet wonderland of the body. He remembers fingering Einstein's heart, and his stomach. He tugged at the white intestines and roped them off, then cut the pericardium and pulmonary artery and separated the trachea and esophagus.

As they often do in a morgue, flies buzzed in the room, but Harvey, lost inside Einstein's body, didn't hear anything. He found nearly three quarts of blood in Einstein's peritoneal cavity, a result of the burst aneurysm, and after further investigation of his heart and veins concluded that, with an operation, the physicist might have lived for several more years, though how long was hard to tell because, according to Harvey, "Einstein liked his fatty foods."

Working under the humming lights, jugging the liver, palpating the heart, Harvey made a decision. Who's to say whether it was inspired by awe or by greed, professional duty or malpractice, beneficence or mere pettiness? Who's to say what comes over a mortal, what chemical reaction takes place, when faced with the blinding brightness of another's greatness, and with it a knowledge that we shall never possess even a cheeseparing of that greatness?

Working quickly with a knife, Harvey tonsured the scalp: slicing from below one of Einstein's ears, around the back of the head to the other ear, and then up and over the crown of the skull in an arcing motion. The skin peeled back from the bone with a ripping sound, like masking tape being pulled quickly from a surface. Harvey again shucked the skin on the face-side so that now the dome of the vanilla-white skull was revealed in its entirety. Bearing down on a buzz saw, he cut through Einstein's head. He cracked the skull like a coconut, he removed a cap of bone, peeled back the viscous meninges, and snipped the connecting blood vessels and nerve bundles and the spinal cord.

And then, at last, there it was. A huge, rough pearl. He reached with his fingers into the chalice of the man's cranium and removed the glistening brain.

2 ◆ No Prisoners

When I was eighteen, a buddy named Mark Paradis and I flew to Oregon and then hitchhiked a couple thousand miles up to Alaska, with the idea of working the fishing boats for a season in a town called Homer. It felt momentous, the prodigal sons setting out to claim their riches. Mark had the hint of a Massachusetts accent and more smarts than three of me combined, and between us we could almost convince ourselves of anything. In pictures taken along the road, we look like kids: me wearing a dopey, squinty-eyed grin; Mark, with a mop of black hair and a wary gaze. By the time we made it to Vancouver, we decided we'd had one too many rides from yahoos drinking Hamm's beer, so we pooled our money and bought a four-hundred-dollar secondhand station wagon that we planned on driving up the Al-Can Highway and right down Fourth Avenue in Anchorage.

Unfortunately for us, we misread the map. The station wagon got us forty miles up a fire road to nowhere, then started rolling backward downhill on a steep incline. "Forty dollars a mile," said Mark, staring blankly through the windshield as we came to a stop on the shoulder and I nodded in disgusted agreement. Stuck, we didn't even get the math right. We sat for several nights by a fire, waiting for someone to drive by. The Saltines ran out, the mosquitoes swarmed, and though we eventually would make it to Alaska (hitchhiking, of course), the memories I treasure most are of those brief but glorious forty miles. I can still remember pulling out of that used-car lot and waving to the salesman, that first-time feeling of cruising under our own power, accelerating up the coast, on a road that for a while ran right along the water. We were hooting and hollering and throwing high fives. We had the windows down, and to our left the ocean glittered like so many newly cut gems. To our right the mountains rose over our shoulders. I'd never been happier.

Five years later, when I was twenty-three, I wanted that feeling back. I quit a job at a Madison Avenue ad agency, where my time had been spent plumbing the depths of the human mind to see if anyone remembered a certain jingle meant to sell a little chocolate bar with crunchy almonds. As my first act of freedom, I drove cross-country with a friend named Bill Mentzer in his brown Alfa Romeo convertible. It was the end of November and cold, and Mentz, a curly-haired, boyish master of several languages, was heading back home to Marin County after a brief and similarly unfulfilling stint in Manhattan. He had an obsessive relationship with his car, as one might with a temperamental foreign lover met on a two-week holiday, and wouldn't dare push it over fifty-five. We drove the entire country in the slow lane, tailgated by menacing grandmothers.

And while our well-being hinged on every cough and tic of that vehicle—and there were many—every day also brought new mystical visions of the kind that belong to all cross-country travelers: Chicago rising out of the Midwest like huge metallic cornstalks, the awe-inspiring, Great Plains splendor of everything past St. Louis, and then Denver appearing in a purple vision before the Rockies. At a diner in the middle of nowhere, we came upon a waitress so pretty it took a moment to summon our courage to order, and one midnight at a haunted bar in Flagstaff, a water pipe broke and the fire in the fireplace flared and everyone fled out the front door, including the bartender himself. Along the road, we crashed with friends or at Motel 6s, victoriously drinking cold beer at the end of each day like two veteran long-haulers, watching late-night talk shows, and by the time we made California we threw the top down and howled like two naked hippies at the moon.

One of the themes of my earlier life, as I recall it now, is that I was forever projecting myself forward and backward at the same time, negating the present moment, changing my mind with alarming frequency. A master of vicissitudes, I fell in and out of love with certain ideas and certain rock bands and certain girlfriends who, in the end, must have been glad to see me go. After all, I couldn't name my longing, and yet it was there, always driving me away from the place where I stood.

My mother's side of our family is a Scotch-Irish clan, with five generations that have lived in the northernmost region of New York State. It is here that half of my history lies. A great-great-grandmother, a Catholic who married into a Protestant family, and who felt so besieged by guilt, God, and her in-laws that she drowned herself and her baby in a cistern. A great-uncle, a good, kindly man, who, after baling hay one day, ate chokecherries, drank a glass of milk, and keeled over dead. My cousin Cindy, who would have been my age but was drowned in a winter creek at the age of five. And my uncle Spencer, Cindy's father, who later died in a freak accident when a tractor suddenly tipped back on him. He was forty-two.

And yet the North Country has always felt like a stomping ground, a land beyond the Adirondacks where I go to take my place among the family line of hermits and farmers and chattering schoolteachers. No one in my family questions my desire, however inchoate or ineffable, because it's partly their desire, too: this need to be self-sufficient and free at all costs. Some weekends, my grandfather would simply disappear out in the barn, tinkering for the duration. For many years, I thought this, too, might be my destiny: weekends in the barn. And a life lived by the seasons—comforted by corn in the summer, apples in the fall, fallow winter fields, and an explosion of barn cats and cows in the spring—seemed idyllic but for one thing: Where were all the people?

And where was *the* person? When I really thought about it, after I'd outrun anybody remotely interested in me, I wondered how I might ever find someone with whom I might happily live.

❀

The first time I met Sara was on the phone. I was in grad school at the University of Michigan, and the director of the writing program asked if I might talk to her, to persuade her to come. When I called just before noon, I actually woke her up. She said it probably seemed weird, but she was a last-semester senior at a liberal-arts college, which meant that the only word in that configuration that mattered now was liberal, as in liberal partying. She and four of her friends had just gotten fish tattoos on their ankles. We had a lot to talk about, though I can't remember what it was we said. I just remember her laugh, a soft husk.

When she arrived in Ann Arbor the next fall, we hardly spoke to each other. I don't know why, if it was bashfulness or busyness, stand-offishness or maybe an unconscious feeling that there was going to be time for that later. I wasn't unaware of her, though. I knew she ran and mountain-biked, had long arms and long fingers and strong shoulders from years of rowing crew. She had green eyes and reddish hair that fell in thick strands past her shoulders, a pretty mouth with pretty lips, a scar beneath her chin, and sometimes, around her friends, she couldn't help herself from laughing, an uncensored schnorting laugh that changed everything about her, lifted her just slightly from the ground. And she had a boyfriend. At various readings by visiting writers, when he came late, they'd kiss and sit close. When he didn't come, she'd drape her legs over the seat in front of her, in a comfortable slouch.

As it was, sometime in the late winter of her second year, we ended up at a party. While everyone was playing charades, four of us bailed out into a snowstorm and mixed it up with snowballs. It started casually, but then I kept getting pelted in the back of the head . . . hard.

Sara! After maybe a half hour of heavy combat, I remember raising my hands in surrender and her standing in all that white downfall, a knot of energy, strands of wet hair matted to her brow, eyes glittering viciously. "Take no prisoners!" she yelled, and fired another right at my forehead. Then we went back to fighting it out until we were too exhausted to lift our arms anymore.

That's when I knew I was a goner.

We became one indivisible weather system. We wore thrift-store sweaters, drank bourbon late at night, and played gin rummy with the ferocity of old ladies. She cut my hair; I changed the oil in her car. And, after getting our degrees, we were broke. There being no question about our togetherness, we moved, following jobs—Ohio, Kentucky, Illinois, New Mexico. We started with only a futon, and tag-saled our way to couches and dressers and bookcases. We worked thankless, no-pay jobs—I edited while Sara wrote scripts for industrial videos about trash compactors. And yet, in those hours away from work, when we fell out into whatever place we lived on a Friday night, or slept late the next morning, there was a rightness about who we were as a couple, of our guaranteed happiness.

During our second summer together—when I was twenty-eight and she was twenty-five—we took off in my pickup truck, perhaps harboring silent suspicions that we were imagining each other, that somewhere out on Interstate 94 one of us would simply vanish. We drove as far as we could, cooking our meals by WhisperLite stove on the tailgate, at rest stops and national parks through North Dakota and Montana and Idaho, camping and hiking, following roads that led nowhere and following them back again, before we ran out of time somewhere in British Columbia and turned home before fall. Even now, though I can't recall certain key details about the trip— did we make it to Wyoming? Was it Omaha where we both bought alpaca hats, our only souvenir of the trip?—I can remember how the light of the country fell on her as she leaned up against the passenger side door and told me stories. I remember how everything kept

opening up to us until she was as real as the good earth of Iowa, and
I wondered if I'd arrived at the beginning of my future.

Recollecting this last road trip, I now realize that my cross country
journeys all occurred in five-year intervals, as if by cosmic intention.
And yet they all came in response to something deep and unknow-
able, some invisible force seeking to wreck, rearrange, or verify a life
I'd set for myself. They came as demarcations and changing points.
And every time, America looked different to me, too, as if by passing
out of myself into the country, I was entering Oz.

In the months prior to meeting Dr. Harvey, I'd fallen into a major
funk. After five years together, Sara and I were increasingly surrounded by people striving for yuppie respectability: marriage,
houses, good paychecks. And even as we were in full rebellion against
yuppie respectability, we too seemed to be drifting in that direction.
Still, we clung to certain ideas of ourselves. Sara dreamed of seeing
the australs of Antarctica, those plumes of bright charged light playing over McMurdo Station during the South Pole's six months of
darkness. And I envisioned myself traipsing through faraway jungles
to find lost cultures. On those occasions when we talked about marriage and kids, it reminded us of everything we hadn't done yet,
places we hadn't seen, people left to meet.

Confused and suddenly suspicious of each other, and not knowing what to do, we just quit our lives, packed up and moved back
East, to Maine, to be closer to our family and friends. To the middle
of nowhere, really, a place near the New Hampshire border where
you couldn't find enough guys to play a game of pickup basketball.
Even as we settled in, Sara, who'd recently signed a book contract,
was traveling the country—and then the world for months—and
after that spent many more months writing about it. There were unexpected deadlines and pressures and she worked so many consecu-
tive hours for so many days, her entire body ached: her back, her
wrists, her head. When her eyes started twitching, the doctor
prescribed a pair of pink-tinted Hillary-Rodham-at-Wellesley

granny glasses that she could only bring herself to wear when I was sleeping, though occasionally I would sneak up to the loft where she worked to find her in a trance, the glasses punched up on the bridge of her nose, reflecting the words on the computer screen, her lips moving with the story. "I feel like I've aged twenty years," she would say, still a year shy of thirty. "What happened to being young?"

And then me: I was a perfect study in uselessness. I was suddenly CEO of a vast empire that consisted of myself and our dog, Trout, a sweet, skinny lab mix who seemed to have as much time on her hands as I did. With Sara's book advance supporting us for a few months, I was taking time to evaluate my prospects, of which there were basically none. I set up a makeshift office in the basement and spent my days reading and then hiking the nearby mountains with Trout. And then I'd come back home, and maybe stack wood or something to make myself look busy until dinner. But really I'd reached a kind of impasse: So was this what life added up to, a man and his dog?

During these months, I visited Dr. Harvey three or four times. Once, when we went for sushi together, Harvey vaguely mentioned that he needed to take care of some business "out West." Before leaving Kansas, he'd had a little fender bender, so there was the matter of meeting with insurance people. And then he said he was hoping to get to California to see several neuroanatomists who'd studied pieces of Einstein's brain. But most important, he wanted to meet Evelyn Einstein, the granddaughter of Albert, who lived in Berkeley. Although he didn't explain why, I assumed he might be facing down some late-in-life desire to resolve the past with the Einstein family once and for all. Or, before his age permanently grounded him, maybe he wanted to hand the brain over to the next of kin.

He mentioned these things to me offhandedly, and I took them in. It was nearly time for me to go, and I was calculating the hours and contemplating the traffic back to Maine, and without hesitation, I blurted, "I could drive you." It surprised even me.

Harvey regarded the mountain of wasabi on his plate with a quizzical expression. He tapped his chopsticks once but then fell so silent that I could feel the sudden weight of my own eager impropriety. I'd crossed a line, proposed a deeper intimacy where perhaps the old doctor wanted none. And what about Sara, what would she say? Harvey chuckled nervously, "Heh-heh." Like two chops of wood.

"Way-ell," he said, "I don't see why not." It was exactly the opposite answer I expected. And yet doped on the incessant music of tinkling harps and a heady shot of tekka maki, we'd somehow resolved that Harvey and Einstein's brain were going to California and that I, the directionless one, was going to drive us there.

3 ✦ The One-Penny Magenta

In photographs from near the end of his life, Einstein can be seen rocking in a chair on the front porch, having a pipe as his terrier, Chico, sits at his feet, or sharing a joke with a guest. He looks, as he almost always looks in such pictures, benevolent, mild-mannered, and bemused. As if he's an old man in an oversized child's body, quickly growing out of his ill-fitting clothes and yet still has that pajamas-in-the-morning lightness, a certain gaiety and pokiness in the crinkled crow's feet at his eyes as he smiles.

It's hard to balance such seeming outward joy with the misery of Einstein's private life, especially when it came to his family. In 1897, at the Swiss Federal Polytechnical School in Zurich, he met and fell in love with his first wife, a fellow student with a congenital limp named Mileva Maric with whom he shared a yen for coffee and sausage. His early letters to her overflow with pet names—my Dollie, my kitten, my beloved witch, my little everything—and professions of love: "Without the thought of you," he wrote her in 1900 at the age of twenty-one, "I would no longer want to live among this sorry herd of humans."

They studied together, enjoyed music. They became friends and then lovers. When a fellow schoolmate of Einstein's questioned Mileva's limp, admitting that he himself could never marry a cripple, Einstein is reported to have replied, "But she has such a lovely voice." Still, their eventual disconnection as a couple was profound. For even as he claimed to be hers, he was far away, in every way. They lived apart for stretches of time. And then he never could embrace the chaos of children, for all that ever mattered to him was his work. After the birth of a daughter, Lieserl, who was apparently put up for adoption before the couple was married, and then two sons—Hans Albert, who went on to become a hydrolics engineer, and Eduard, who was institutionalized with schizophrenia—Einstein found himself courting his second wife, a cousin named Elsa. In a 1913 letter to her, more than five years before his divorce from Mileva became official, he wrote, "I treat my wife as an employee whom one cannot fire. I have my own bedroom and avoid being with her. . . . I'm absolutely my own master as well as my own wife."

Later, with Elsa, a woman who never bothered with her husband's science nor desired any semblance of intellectual parity, he would repeat himself. A state of sexless lovelessness came between them, and soon the scientist was working on other pretty women "as a magnet acts on iron filings," according to one friend. Again he kept a separate bedroom, and again it seems his wife was reduced to no more than an employee, albeit one who was permitted to accompany him on foreign trips and to movie premieres. "Talk of you or me," he told her, "but never of 'us.' "

In later years, he became embittered toward women, considering the concept of love as altogether spurious, and the theory of lifetime commitment as something worse. "Marriage is the unsuccessful attempt to make something lasting out of an incident," he told Otto Nathan, his friend and the man who became the executor of his estate.

And if Einstein felt himself besieged at home, there were also intense pressures in his public life. As he had been in Germany, Einstein became a popular target in America: for Bible-beaters and Catholic bishops who felt his theories about the origins of the universe undermined God, suggesting a universe in which even morals were relative; for anti-Semites who despised the fact that a Jew like Einstein was such a superstar; for a group of American women patriots, who protested Einstein's 1932 request for an American visa, claiming he was a Communist ("Never before," wrote Einstein, "have I experienced from the fair sex such energetic rejection of all advances; or if I have, then certainly never from so many at once"). And, most of all, for the U.S. government.

FBI files compiled during Einstein's twenty-two-year American sojourn reveal that a slew of federal agents exhaustively followed up on any number of outrageous claims made against Einstein during the 1940s and 1950s. At various times, agents reported that the great scientist was allegedly building robots that could read the minds of our top military leaders, seriously plotting with the Hollywood glitterati to overthrow the U.S. government, or working as a secret agent for Joseph Stalin with plans to emigrate to the Soviet Union.

In one FBI memo from Agent V. P. Keay to H. B. Fletcher quoting information culled from a newspaper article, Keay reported: "In May, 1948, Professor Einstein and 'ten former Nazi research braintrusters' held a secret meeting at which they put on asbestos suits. . . ." According to the agent, the men then watched as a beam of light was fired from a laser gun, melting a block of steel. "[T]his new and secret weapon," he wrote, "could be operated from planes to destroy entire cities." By comparison, the atomic bomb would seem like "little boy's stuff." J. Edgar Hoover, in a fit of outrage, issued a brisk memo to the Army declaring that he was investigating Albert Einstein for the "possible revocation of his citizenship."

Looking back now, of course, the whole episode seems utterly absurd. But in the FBI's rush to prove Einstein's treachery, in the Red Scare days of the midcentury, the reports, issued by agents from Newark to Tucson to Los Angeles, reached ever new ludicrous heights. And yet, in the hypercharged atmosphere that often enveloped the physicist, the most amazing claims against Einstein, however overblown and specious, had a way of sticking as fact. What was to be most feared about the genius was invisible: his superhuman mental powers. Even then, the government wanted control of Einstein's brain.

⚛

On a cold winter day, during one of my early visits to Dr. Harvey, we drove around Princeton, making the obligatory pilgrimage to 112 Mercer Street, the house where Einstein spent the last twenty years of his life. We sat for a while with the car running, warm air pouring from the heater, gazing at a modest wood-frame colonial with black shutters on a pleasant block of like houses. More than anything, Einstein said he loved the old place for the light that filled the upstairs rooms and for the gardens out back. He kept pictures of Michelangelo and Schopenhauer hanging in his study, because, as he said, both men had escaped an everyday life of raw monotony and taken "refuge in a world crowded with images of our own creation."

Sitting in the car, Thomas Harvey recalled how the Einstein family gathered here after the scientist's death, how his son Hans Albert, and Einstein's longtime assistant, Helen Dukas, and Einstein's executor, Otto Nathan, as well as a small group of intimates, drove to a secret spot along the Delaware River and scattered the ashes that remained of Albert Einstein's body. And that was it.

Not surprisingly, however, controversy immediately enshrouded the removal of Einstein's brain. Word was leaked by Harvey's former teacher Dr. Zimmerman that Harvey had Einstein's brain, and that he, Zimmerman, was expecting to receive it from his student. When this was reported in *The New York Times* a day after Einstein's death, Hans Albert, who knew nothing about his father's brain having been removed, was flabbergasted. Otto Nathan expressed regret and shock, and later implied that Harvey was a bald-faced thief. But according to Harvey, Nathan, who died in 1984, stood by the door of the morgue, watching the entire autopsy. (Nathan would later claim he didn't know what Harvey was up to.)

Meanwhile, Harvey announced in a press conference that he was

planning to conduct medical research on the brain. He says he spoke
to Hans Albert over the phone, assuring him that the brain would be
studied for its scientific value, which would then be reported in a
medical journal, thus allaying one of the deepest fears of the Einstein
family: that the brain would become a pop-cultural gewgaw. "My one
regret is that I didn't come here to Mercer Street and talk to Hans
Albert in person," Harvey told me that day. "You know, clear things
up before it got out of hand."

But things were already out of hand. Zimmerman, then on staff at
New York's Montefiore Medical Center, prepared for the delivery of
Einstein's brain, but it never arrived. Increasingly flummoxed, then
angry and embarrassed, Zimmerman found out that Princeton
Hospital, under the direction of a man named John Kauffman, had
decided not to relinquish it. "Hospitals Tiff over Brain of Einstein,"
read one 1955 headline, and went on to describe how the brain remained at "the center of a jurisdictional dispute," with Princeton
Hospital standing its ground, like an old-time gunfighter, claiming
"the brain wouldn't be taken out of town."

But then, a few years after the autopsy, Harvey was fired from his
job for allegedly refusing to give up Einstein's brain to Kauffman. In
fact, Harvey had kept the brain himself, not at the hospital but at
home, and when he left Princeton he simply took it with him. Years
passed. There were no studies or findings. And, in turn, no legal action was brought against Harvey, as there was no precedent in the
courts for the recovery of a brain under such circumstances. And
then Harvey fell off the radar screen. When he gave an occasional in-
terview—in local newspaper articles from 1956 and 1979 and 1988—
he always repeated that he was about "a year from finishing study on
the specimen."

Four decades later, there's still no study. And because somewhere
in his watery blue eyes, his genial stumble-footing, and that ineffable
cloak of hunched integrity that falls over the old, I find myself feeling for him and can't bring myself to ask the essential questions: Is

he a grave-robbing thief or a renegade? A sham artist or a shaman? What about rumors that he plans to sell Einstein's brain to Michael Jackson for some unspecified millions of dollars   or has entertained another private offer of $3 million? Does he feel ashamed or justified? If the brain is the ultimate Fabergé egg, the Hope Diamond, the Cantino Map, the One-Penny Magenta stamp, what does it look like? Feel like? Smell like? Does he talk to it as one talks to one's poodle or ferns?

Once, on my third or fourth visit, I asked if I might see the infamous brain for myself. Dr. Harvey hemmed and hawed, hoping perhaps that I might forget my own question. Then he relented, arranging to take me to a secret location maybe ten miles from his house, one he asked that I not reveal. He had me sit on a couch in an ill-lit room and then disappeared. The room was hot, and it didn't help that I was wearing my wool hunting jacket. Still, Harvey had made it clear that I shouldn't get comfy: We wouldn't be long. I could hear him shuffling up and down some stairs, then struggling with something heavy. He was panting and making a soft sound that would later become familiar: the gumming and light smacking of his lips. One of Harvey's sons was there, too—a son from Harvey's first marriage—a handsome, polite, fit man of about forty whose presence seemed meant to dissuade me from any crazy ideas. He stood silently in the shadows, watching, seemingly a bit bored. He knew the drill.

Harvey appeared from the darkness with a big cardboard box in his hands. He set it down, and one at a time pulled out two large glass cookie jars full of what looked to be chunks of chicken in a golden broth: Einstein's brain chopped into pieces ranging from the size of a turkey neck to a dime. A swirling universe unto itself: galaxies, suns, and planets. It seemed to glow. And the old man, he stood over it, transfixed, nodding. In his face was a sudden nakedness, an expression of awe, of the soul manifesting itself on the surface of the body.

And then he noticed me, noticing. Perhaps he saw my fascination, too, or maybe he was mad at himself for revealing so much; for after all, Dr. Thomas Harvey had spent these last decades invisible to most of the world. He immediately gathered the cookie jars back up, returned them to the box, and Quasimodoed from the room, leaving me nothing but the aftervision. Flashes of bright light. The chill of a visitation.

When he returned, he seemed a little sheepish. "Way-ell," he said, chuckling nervously, "it sure has been a wonderful specimen." Then he would say no more.

4 ♦ Three for the Road

On the day I left to start cross-country with Dr. Harvey, Sara drove me to the bus in Portland. It was gray and snowing. We didn't say good-bye really; we just stood on the sidewalk for a while and then hugged. But between my hunting jacket and her layers of sweaters, I couldn't feel her anymore. She was going back to her book, and I was going . . . well, I wasn't exactly sure where I was going. But I was going. It was February and snowing and her ears were red and Trout was maniacally licking the ice. I can't say for sure whether she wanted me to come back. And I can't say I knew I would.

Sometimes moments like this don't make any sense when you're in them. It's only later, when you remember back, that they stand as a dividing line between who you were and what you've become. And though there are no words to describe what you feel at the time, you don't know what most matters until you've stood on a street corner in front of an idling bus and parted with someone and gotten on that bus to begin a journey with a man who has Einstein's brain. Until you've watched her through the window, getting in the car that the two of you share, the one with dog nose-prints on the inside windshield, mistakenly setting the wipers off on cue—and then watched as she pulls away, taillights blurring in traffic, the bus moving away from that spot where she last was. No, the strange thing is you can't say what you felt in the split second that you felt it—and how that changed everything after—until time leads you back to that moment again in the future.

The February day never gave up its gray, never seemed to offer an iota of mercy. I tried not to think about the future, just made my mind settle on where it was. The bus was warm and yet I still felt cold. There was a pale, haggard woman with a two-pack hacking cough in a nearby seat, probably around my age actually, but looking decades older. Still, she had pretty eyes, big spooky blue, and I wondered what had brought her to this bus—and where was she going. And the guy with a spiderweb tattoed to the back of his neck, wearing only a T-shirt in this zero-degree weather. And the old woman in the front seat, clutching her purse, as if she were among beggars and thieves in Harare. You could see their lives on their faces: They all looked so worried and afraid. Did I, too?

At South Station, in Boston, I picked up a couple of doughnuts, grabbed a few newspapers, and went down to the trains. My plan was to go to Connecticut, stay the night at my parents' house, rent a car, and then start out for Princeton the next morning to pick up Dr. Harvey and the brain. I was wearing faded cargo pants, my plaid hunting jacket, and some scuffed-up work boots. I had a single bag for the journey packed with a pair of jeans, a couple of flannel shirts, T-shirts, a sweater or two, shorts for when the weather turned warm, some underwear, and socks. Had it not been for the bunch of books and the fleeting well-launderedness of my belongings, everything I had could have been wrapped in a sheet, tied to a pole, and passed as a hobo's.

The train was a comfort. Even walking the platform, listening to the engine belch and hiss, made me happy, the rails reeling out in silver lines to somewhere else. I've always loved the train ride from Boston to my parents'. Loved it for the same reasons I've come to covet long flights to foreign places or the memory of car trips our family used to take north from Connecticut, up through the Adirondacks—through Lake Placid, Saranac Lake, and St. Regis

Falls—to our grandparents' in Potsdam, New York. For those moments in transit when you ride in the bubble of your own thoughts,
without intrusion, moving at sixty, seventy, eighty miles an hour,
when everything becomes color and speed and, for a moment, you
outrace your woes. Moving through space like this, it's easier to
imagine, as Einstein once did, what it might feel like to ride a beam
of light.

On board, there were nothing but easterners: cashmere-sweatered
students on their way from Harvard to Yale for a debating contest,
businesspeople with briefcases and laptop computers, well-dressed
older folks off on a museum trip to Manhattan. These were train
people with their subdued bonhomie rather than bus people with
their naked desperation. The train barreled down through Rhode
Island, hugging the coast, and brought us to the water by Mystic. I
marked the Atlantic in my mind—the green-gray sheen of it, its
moody, inward beauty—for by the time Dr. Harvey and I reached the
Pacific Ocean, whenever that was, I knew nothing would be the same.
And if we never made California? Well, then, our destiny lay somewhere between here and there, in some landlocked town we'd not yet
heard of, among people whose faces we'd not yet seen.

❈

Since leaving home just after college, I've returned on holidays and
random weekends over the years, never really staying more than a few
nights, just enough time to catch up with my friends and family before caroming back into the world. Each time, I find myself searching
the manicured landscape of my suburbia, as one might the face and
gestures and intonations of a long-lost brother for clues as to who you
must be. And then, of course, the winding roads and snaking stone
walls, the beaches and swimming pools, are a map of my entire youth:
my greatest mistakes and my most minute, sweet victories. There's the
Little League baseball field where I played catcher as a kid, emulating
my only hero, the great Yankee catcher Thurman Munson, who died

in a plane crash in 1979 at roughly the same age I am now. There's the graveyard of my first kiss. There are houses, inhabited today by new families living new lives, in which my best friends once lived, where we might have wiled away hours playing Whiffle ball or football. When I pass those homes, I occasionally see a man out front raking leaves or cutting the grass—tan and trim and khaki-clad—a man who could be a father from my past, smelling faintly of gin, but now is simply someone who is a different variation of me, had I stayed in this town and kept a job in Manhattan.

When I came off the train, my father was already there, waiting, wearing a baseball cap, his compact, muscly self bundled in a tan jacket. He's retired now, and being retired he gets to do the things that time never afforded him during the busy years. Like cook and run errands and pick people up who need picking up. I'd traveled 250 miles, as nothing but a passenger, but already felt spent. I ate with my parents: grilled swordfish, asparagus, new potatoes. "This could be your last meal for a while," my mother said, smiling as if she knew something I didn't. But she and my father kept stealing glances at me, perhaps confused or worried, I don't know. I just ate until I felt as if I might burst. And then some more. Afterward, maps were laid out on the table, possible cross-country routes were traced by fingertip. The Weather Channel was consulted, the television screen flickering with winter storms and snow-blown, whited-out interstates. "Could be tough-going," said my father gravely. "Any chance you can put it off until spring?"

I'd told my parents about Dr. Harvey and Einstein's brain, though I'm certain it hadn't entirely registered. Or maybe they just didn't want to know too much. Through my various flights of ridiculous fancy, they've learned the fine art of encouragement without asking too many questions. "Are you going to be safe?" asked my mom.

"Keep your eyes open," said my dad. "You don't know what kind of funny business you might run into out there."

We sat up for a while talking. My parents asked about Sara, and I told them she was fine, we were fine, all was fine, for to have told them otherwise would have made them worry. My mom filled me in on the latest doings about town, and my dad, ever hopeful, laid out master plans for the backyard, how a few spirea bushes and some perennials would give a whole new shape and form to the bosky extravaganza out there come spring. I went upstairs around ten, lay down in my childhood bed, in the back room I had shared with one of my three brothers. On the surface ours had been one of those most normal American households—sports and good grades and nice friends. Growing up, there was never a moment's silence. Even falling asleep at night we'd talk until the other was snoring, or later, as teenagers, we'd just listen to Pink Floyd's *Animals* or Van Morrison's *Astral Weeks* until the music exited us into some psychedelic dream.

But now there was silence, deep and unbroken. It occurred to me that I was on the verge of a very strange departure. And then I slept.

The next morning, before I left, the three of us went to the beach for one of my mother's signature "speed walks," her version of Olympic walking in which she throws an occasional flurry of punches at the air. There was a threatening sky, and a cold, hard wind clipped some last leaves from the pin oaks that stand sentinel along the edge of Long Island Sound. Out of nowhere, my dad started talking to me about velocity. And about mortality. Normally that kind of talk would have made me uncomfortable, but it came up so quickly and naturally—like its own gust of wind—that I just let it in. "When you're young, time takes forever," he said. "Then, it starts flying. And suddenly, you'd give anything for ten more years."

He said this as my mother was out ahead of us, but then we rallied and gained on her again. For years, I've come home searching for signs of encroaching old age in them—noting new gray hairs, wrinkles, and lapses in memory. Their mortality is my constant fear, the specter of their passing my constant denial, and yet, now they both looked young and vibrant. From the side, my mother was seemingly seventeen, her face flushed, a small-town girl on her way to becoming a schoolteacher, the wind luffing her thick, short dark hair, something expectant and optimistic in her gaze. Beneath his sweatshirt hood, my father was a wrestler again, rock-hard and undefeated in his senior high-school year, a Big Ten scholarship, a future job with a blue-chip computer company, and the whole rest of his life laid out before him, his four boys still a fantastic abstraction.

Later, they drove me to the car rental in White Plains. We hugged good-bye, and my mom gave her usual good-luck admonition, "Be careful!" My dad, he looked as if he had a question on his mind, but then never asked it. The rental car was a teal-colored, four-door Skylark. Not my first choice, but good enough. There were eighty-seven miles on the odometer. I threw my bag in the trunk, turned the key in the ignition, and by habit riffled over the radio stations as I started to drive, all these voices suddenly speaking to me. I don't know why, but hearing them just made me feel good.

Manhattan was flecked gray. I slid out over the dun-colored swamps of the Meadowlands dotted by popsicle-orange pools of sludge. Planes came and went overhead from Newark Airport, and it seemed that everyone in the world had some busy intention, some place they had to have been three minutes ago.

I was one of them, too. Off the Jersey Turnpike, I gassed the Skylark through exurbia, through swirls of dead leaves and unruly thickets of oak and pine that gave way again to well-ordered fields with horses. I passed a barn with a handmade sign that read Smitty's Deer Butchering, wiggled left up a hill, peaked the crown beneath a few early, late-afternoon stars, then cruised down its backside. There was the inclined drive, and hidden among trees, the ranch again.

Before I could get out of the car, Dr. Harvey was shuffling down the front stairs, a tier of cement steps, raring to go. Had he been waiting all this while by the kitchen door? Instead of Pendleton tie and suspenders, he was a man transformed by his road duds: a buckskin-colored jacket, a blue turtleneck, and a pair of jeans with a Calvin Klein label. The green beret sat jauntily askew on his head, the Beat hipster rising out of retirement for the last great tea-and-bongo rally.

Watching him, I felt two equal and nearly opposite things: joy and apprehension. Joy that we were almost gone. And apprehension, because I was truly worried. What if he got sick, or slipped on something and broke his hip? Who'd believe I hadn't had it in for him? In one hand, he carried a plaid suitcase rimmed with fake leather; in the other sagged a heavy gray duffel. He moved in almost exaggerated motion, as if the hand of some puppeteer were controlling the strings, yanking him in a slight herky-jerky.

When he reached me, he dropped his bags and extended a hand. We shook, Harvey's mouth in an iguana smile that kind of drifted right by me—we caught each other out of the corner of our eyes as he passed—and then he came back again, as if we'd just greeted each other on the deck of a ship in particularly heavy seas, which, I realized, was a function of his accident-shortened leg.

"Way-ell," he said. "How was the drive?"

But he didn't wait for an answer, didn't even let me offer help. Hoisted his bags and made a beeline for the car. His girlfriend, Cleora, followed him down the stairs in a blue bathrobe. She had a thin, pretty face and auburn hair. Cleora had met Harvey when she was a nurse at Princeton Hospital back in the 1950s. Now they were together. "Oh my, as you can see, he's been waiting all afternoon," she said, her voice a purr. On my previous visits, she'd made herself scarce, but now she was permitted to preside over her boyfriend's departure. "He's worried about me," she confided.

"Why's that?" I asked.

She lowered her voice. "I have a little GI upset." A beat passed, and she registered my confusion. "You know, *gastrointestinal*." She vaguely pointed downward.

"I'll be okay," said Cleora bravely, smiling at Dr. Harvey, who lifted his luggage in the trunk next to mine, fussed with things for a moment, then slammed the hatch shut. He came back and pecked her good-bye.

"Good-bye, sweetie," he said.

"He's a fine Quaker gentleman," she told me, watching Harvey's curled-over self shuffle back across the pavement. He rubbed a smudge of dirt off my side mirror, then toodled around the front of the car. She sighed. "Yes," she said, "he's always tried to do the right thing.

"Take good care of him," she called after me, and I promised I would. Once inside the car, seated and situated, Harvey buckled. I buckled. Harvey exhaled, I exhaled.

"All set?" I asked.

"Sure," he said.

"You got the brain?" I asked.

"In the duffel," he said.

We looked at each other once, then I turned the ignition. The engine kicked to life. Harvey chuckled nervously, scratchily cleared his throat, and uttered what would become his mantra, "Yessir . . . real good." He took the map in his hand and seemed to examine California closely as we backed past Cleora, who was airily waving good-bye, and down the driveway. And then we just started on our way. Yes, everything was already moving. All that would happen already had. We just gave ourselves up to it, and let ourselves slip in.

Part Two

5 ◆ Warp and Wobble

We begin in silence, each of us adjusting to the new conditions of our capsule existence, like *Apollo* astronauts. Weeks of anticipation begin their slow melt under the bright sodium-light reality of barreling eighteen-wheelers, zoomy starling cars, and what will be four thousand miles of dizzying white line. But for one moment, running alongside the Delaware River, twisting through dark winter trees, burbling with the same gray-blue currents into which Einstein's ashes were supposedly sprinkled after his death, we're American newborns.

Being the driver, my responsibilities are vast: gas, oil, air in the tires, the removal of dead bugs from the windshield, the monitoring of all engine lights, the timely dispensation of miles to our next destination, the ultimate comfort of my passenger. It is my charge at every self-serve station to get out and inspect our vehicle, to walk one full revolution around it in a grave manner, sharply considering, as if we were about to join a military review in Red Square. Also, I command the radio and have my tapes for the moments when Harvey nods off, which I suspect will be often. And selecting the right tapes for the right parts of the country has been no easy feat. I packed and repacked my tape box over and over, trying to predict what music I'll need to get me through. I've got everything from Soul Coughing and Pavement to Hank Williams and Lightning Hopkins. Still, my greatest fear remains that I will reach for Son Volt in Missouri or Buddy Holly in Texas, and the tape just won't be there.

Our route has been a matter of some internal debate between me and myself. Owing to the approach of the mean winter storms that my father spotted on the Weather Channel, I've decided we'll take the straightest path between here and Lawrence, Kansas—I-70 as it runs through Columbus and Indianapolis and St. Louis. From there, Harvey and I have discussed the idea of getting off the interstate and dipping down through the Southwest, on to Las Vegas and Los Angeles, before heading north again to San Francisco. And yet Harvey remains enigmatic on the issue. When I ask if he'd rather see Salt Lake City or Los Alamos, he says, "Oh sure, that'd be nice." When I ask the same question a little louder this time, he says, "Way-ell, real good."

The inside of the Skylark already looks like an unruly bachelor pad. Strewn here and there are seltzer bottles and Stoned Wheat Thins, a case for sunglasses and a half-eaten roll of Life Savers. And the back foot well fills with a growing pile of trash, including the pink and blue tissuey copies of the rental agreement, the remnants of my earlier deli lunch crumpled in a brown bag, and an empty Coke can. It's a trend that will continue—somewhere in Ohio, Harvey will leave his good manners behind. After he polishes off a doughnut and a half-pint of milk, I'll watch him toss the carton over his left shoulder as if he's been doing it for a lifetime.

But now he sits, hunched like a frog, his green beret slightly askew, blinking softly in the approaching twilight. To be sure, Harvey is my kind of passenger: a low-maintenance, up-for-anything argonaut. The good doctor takes to the road like it's a river of fine brandy, growing stronger on its oily fumes and oily-rainbow mirages, its oily fast food and the oily-tarmacked gas plazas that we skate across for candy bars while the Skylark feeds at the pump.

And the brain? Some portion of it rides in the trunk. But how much, I'm not exactly sure. When I spoke to Harvey by phone before leaving, he'd said he'd fished a few fistfuls of it from his cookie jars and sealed the payload in Tupperware, which he then zipped in the duffel bag. And now the thought of it sitting back there, sloshing around in formaldehyde, seems so impossible and distracting that, for these first miles, I'm not at my Andretti best on the road.

We arrive in Philadelphia at rush hour. To pick up the westbound interstate, we exit onto city streets for several blocks, passing near the University of Pennsylvania, a cluster of brick buildings behind black gates. And though he says nothing about it, I'll later learn that this tangle of streets, this short trip from Princeton to Philadelphia, is one that Harvey knows well from the days just after he came into possession of Einstein's brain. Having entrusted himself to lead a study of the brain, Harvey visited the university to have slides made of Einstein's thalamus.

I glance once at the old man, a portrait of contented complacency. Nothing about him betrays how many people would love to find Harvey in their crosshairs. Even Hebrew University in Jerusalem, the beneficiary of Einstein's estate, has raised the possibility of trying to claim the brain, as it once claimed a cache of his papers, which were kept at the Institute for Advanced Study in Princeton. Freeman Dyson, a famous scientist in his own right and a member of the Institute, remembered the incident in the preface of a book about Einstein as if it were a piece of detective fiction:

> It was a dark and rainy night. A large truck stood in front of the Institute with a squad of well-armed Israeli soldiers standing guard. . . . In quick succession, a number of big wooden crates were brought down in the elevator from the top floor, carried out of the building through the open front door, and loaded onto the truck. The soldiers jumped on board and the truck drove away into the night. The next day, the archive was in its final resting place in Jerusalem.

Recalling Dyson's words, I find myself inadvertently checking the rearview for an Israeli Hummer, but find only a low-rider with bright silver hubcaps. At the wheel is an unshaven, hard-looking gang-banger type with a bandana tied on his head like a pirate. As he accelerates past us, there's a message scrawled on his back window, in white soap that will probably vanish with the first hard rain: R.I.P. Tito, My Beloved Dog. Something about that offers the first heartbreak of the road, for surely, in better days, with Tito by his side, a wake of broken noses and chomped rear ends trailed behind this man. Even as Harvey doesn't seem to notice, I wonder: What kind of pooch was this Tito and what did he mean to that lonely man?

※

Pennsylvania is its own kind of in-between, not really east and not west, the pulse between neurons. Once beyond Philadelphia, the state opens into hills and mountains and broad, flat valleys. There's still a little light in the sky—swirls of violet—and Harvey greedily gathers the landscape through his wondering blue eyes. Across fields, we can mark the presence of people coming home from work by the lights turning on in their kitchens and the glow of television light in the family rooms. We pass over the Susquehanna River, dark and flowing with broken, pale-specked stars, up Blue Mountain, which is now black, and we lose civilization for a while. And then Harvey is talking, recalling many, many years ago taking blood in this area from one Mr. Lambert, of Listerine mouthwash fame—yes, taking blood at the man's mansion, then being served breakfast, and creeping back across the front lawn with vials full of plasma.

He remembers Grace Kelly, how she grew up in Philadelphia—"a real Pennsylvania girl!"—and claims Eisenhower had a farm in these parts, too, somewhere. He seems to mistake his proximity in age to these now-vanished people for intimacy—or perhaps in his relative universe, they *are* intimates. He refers to them on a first name basis: "Of course, Grace went to Monte Carlo and became a princess . . ."

On these subjects, Harvey can be downright loquacious, stringing the life of one famous figure to the next. Unprovoked, he offers this synopsis of his favorite author: "Well, Kay Boyle fell in love with a French boy and they went to France but his family was very strict and she convinced him to go to Paris. Well, yes, heh heh, I'd say she liked it quite a bit there. When it was time to go, the French boy had to leave alone. See, Kay had fallen in love with an American boy! He later died, dropped dead of something, and so she moved to Italy and fell in love with an Austrian boy, a skier I think he was. Well, she was an active girl and eventually she moved back to California and worked with that Chavez fellow on farm issues. Oh yes, she's someone I would have liked to meet. Yessir, whatta life!"

There's no mention of her stories, just her lovers, as if she is more distinguished in Harvey's eyes for the danger and adventure and freewheeling affairs of her life than for her writing. When the topic turns to Einstein's brain, however, he clams up. He speaks in a clipped, spare, almost penurious way—with a barely perceptible drawl from his Kentucky childhood—letting time fall between the subject and the verb, and then all the words after. When I ask why it's taken more than four decades to release a comprehensive study of Einstein's brain, he chuckles flatly, raspily clears his throat, then says, "Way-ell . . ." And just steps aside to let some more time pass, returning to the atlas, which he studies as if it's a rune.

I don't press the issue. Instead, I turn my attention to the radio, tuning in all kinds of high-school basketball, gardening shows, local on-air auctions, blathering DJs, farm reports, and Christian call-in shows. I've got my cache of music, just waiting for Harvey to nod off, as well as a book on tape, *Neuromancer* by William Gibson, a sci-fi classic about a violent world in which shadowy agents deal in genetic materials and synthetic glandular extract, where the perfectly cloned and grafted human being is a thing of the present.

Despite my expectations that Harvey will blink off into poppy-laden sleep, what I soon realize is that he's damn perky for eighty-four. Hours pass, and he watches the last of Pennsylvania: its barns and elaborate hexes, signs for Amish goods, the Allegheny Mountains rising like dark whales out of the earth. He watches night come down in purples, silvers, and cinnamons, like the plush, sequined curtain on some midnight talk show. And then half of Ohio passes in the night, all pan-flattened and thrown back down on itself. He blinks languidly at it, but never sleeps.

A confession: I want Harvey to sleep. I want him to fall into a deep, blurry, Rip Van Winkle daze, and I want to park the Skylark mother-ship and walk around to the trunk and open it. I want Harvey snoring loudly as I unzip the duffel bag and reach my hands inside, and I want to—what?—touch Einstein's brain. I want to touch the brain. Yes, I've admitted it. I want to hold it, coddle it, measure its weight in my palm, handle some of its one hundred billion now-dormant neurons. Does it feel like tofu, sea urchin, bologna? What, exactly? And what does such a desire make me? One of the legion of relic freaks? Or something worse?

The more the idea persists in my head, the more towns slip past outside the window as Harvey gazes into the distant living rooms of happy families, the more I wonder what, in fact, I'd be holding if I held the brain. I mean, it's not really Einstein and it's not really a brain, but disconnected pieces of a brain, just as the passing farms are not really America but parts of a whole, symbols of the thing itself, which is everything and nothing at once.

Still, I'd be touching Einstein the Superstar, immediately recognizable by the electrocuted hair and those mournful, mirthful eyes. The man whose American apotheosis is so complete that he's now a coffee mug, a postcard, a T-shirt. A figure of speech, an ad pitchman, a bumper sticker ("I'm hung like Einstein," reads one that I spy on the back of some ironic VW Jetta, "and I'm smart as a horse"). Despite the fact that he was a sixty-one-year-old man when he was naturalized as an American citizen, it's amazing how fully he's been appropriated by this country.

But why? I think the answer is that, more so than anyone else in the last one hundred years, Einstein was not exactly one of us. Even now, he comes back again as both Lear's fool and Tiresias, comically offering his uncanny vision of the future while warning us about the lurking violence of humankind. "I do not know how the third world war will be fought," he is said to have cautioned, "but I do know how the fourth will: with sticks and stones." Because he glimpsed into the workings of the universe and saw an impersonal God—what he called an "invisible piper"—and because he greeted the twentieth century by rocketing into the twenty-first with his breakthrough theories, he assumed a mien of invincibility. And because his sloppy demeanor stood in such stark contrast to what we expect from a white-winged prophet, he seemed both innocent and trustworthy, and thus that much more supernatural.

If we've incorporated the theory of relativity into our scientific view of the universe, as well as our literature, art, music, and culture at large, it's the great scientist's attempt to devise a kind of personal religion—an intimate spiritual and political manifesto—that still stands in stark, almost sacred contrast to the Pecksniffian systems of salvation offered by modern society. Einstein's blending of twentieth-century skepticism with nineteenth-century romanticism offers a different kind of hope.

"I am a deeply religious nonbeliever," he said. "This is a somewhat new kind of religion." Pushing further, he sought to marry science and religion by redefining their terms. "I am of the opinion that all the finer speculations in the realm of science spring from a deep religious feeling," he said. "I also believe that this kind of religiousness . . . is the only creative religious activity of our time."

To touch Einstein's brain, then, would be to ride a ray of light, as Einstein once dreamed it as a child. To clasp time itself. To feel the warp and wobble of the universe. Einstein claimed that the happiest thought of his life came to him in 1907, during his seven-year tenure at the Patent Office in Bern, when he was twenty-eight and still couldn't find a teaching job. Up to his ears in a worsted-wool suit and patent applications, a voice in his mind whispered, "If a person falls freely, he won't feel his own weight." That became the general theory of relativity. His life and ideas continue to fill thousands of books; even today, scientists are still verifying his work. Recently, a NASA satellite took millions of measurements in space that proved a uniform distribution of primordial temperatures just above absolute zero; that is, the data proved that the universe was in a kind of post-coital afterglow from the big bang, further confirming Einstein's explanation for how the universe began.

It would be good to touch that.

❄

We disembark that first night at a Best Western in Columbus, Ohio. We emerge into the cold night air and stretch and look up at the kind of instantaneous, stucco-and-plywood structures that comprise the highway oases pods of this country. Our home for a night. As we open the trunk to gather our bags, I watch Harvey take what he needs, then leave the gray duffel there, the zipper shining like silver teeth in the streetlight.

"Is it safe?" I ask, nodding my head toward the duffel.

"Is what safe?" Harvey asks back, gelid eyes sparking once in the dark. He doesn't seem to know or remember. Could it be that he's carried the gray matter for so long he now considers himself the important one? No longer defined by the specimen, he's become the specimen. A piece of living history. On tour like a rock star. In his glen-paid suitcase, he carries a pile of postcards that he recently had made of himself, a photograph in which he sits pensively, posed like Rodin's Thinker.

Harvey refuses my help with his luggage, shoulders the duffeled brain, and carries it up the stairs to his room. I see him in, then retreat next door to my own room. Our first night together on the road and I'm bushed. I pull the gaudy bedspread from one of the queens, load extra pillows on it, muss the room according to my own specifications: an open bag, tossed books, strewn socks. To leave some temporary signature on a room that, by our departure tomorrow, will carry no memory of me.

I floss and brush my teeth and catch myself in the mirror, like so many other sorry souls in motel rooms across America at this very moment. I remember that after more than eight million people had marched to their deaths in the fields of Europe during World War I, Einstein's theory of relativity allowed humanity, in the words of one of the scientist's colleagues, to look up from an "earth covered with graves and blood to the heavens covered with the stars." He suddenly appeared on the world's doorstep, inspiring pan-national awe and reconciliation—a liberal German Jew who clung to his Swiss citizenship and renounced violence. What better way to absolve one's self of all sins than to follow a blameless scientist up into the glimmering waters of time and space?

At home, my parents have shoe boxes full of pictures of my brothers and me, an incriminating gallery that captures each of us in our most celebrated and awkward phases of growing up. My brother Steve, a chubby-cheeked Buddha, clad in green Christmas knickers and stockings before a lighted tree; my brother John in his various combinations of black eyes, fat lips, and stitches from playing football or running headfirst into trees; and in shot after shot, my brother Rich, the youngest, looking like Curious George, a big, beaming smile and little monkey ears.

As for me, there's a picture that my parents like to trot out of a wiggly-butted, bald newborn fresh from the hospital, naked on the changing table, looking at the camera with a stunned, watery gaze. Because I was their first child, my parents took more than a few of these snapshots, but the baby featured in them always vaguely reminded me of someone else. In a family of brown eyes and brown hair, I grew into the oddball with blue eyes and blond hair. A running joke among my high school friends was that I looked suspiciously like the garbageman. But that's not who I saw when that pruney baby stared back at me.

When I was twenty-six, my grandfather was dying of Alzheimer's in a Burlington, Vermont, hospital. He'd been a big guy with broad shoulders and tremendous hands that, when made into fists, seemed like granite blocks to my brothers and me. Now he'd lost maybe fifty pounds. Shadows filled his temples, his skin turned sallow, even his fingers seemed slender and breakable. The last time that I saw him alive at the age of eighty-three, he had those same bewildered blue eyes that I'd had as a newborn.

But here's the thing about my grandfather: I think he had no intention of dying. He'd always lived in his body rather than his head. He hunted and fished. He'd grown up working on the family farm and then in a quarry and finally as a lineman for the electric company. "He liked people," my grandmother once told me. "He just didn't like to show it." And he liked dogs, too, but then that was easier: a scratched ear, a tossed bone. In fact, he was never without a dog, and the dog was called one of two names: Prince or Pal. Prince would grow old and pass on and the next day he'd go to the pound and pick out another mutt and name it Pal. His whole life he had only two dogs—Prince and Pal, in dutiful rotation. That was how he beat back time. That was how he made an afterlife on Earth.

Another contemporary of Einstein's, Erwin Schrödinger, claimed that Einstein's theory of relativity quite simply meant "the dethronement of time as a rigid tyrant," opening up the possibility that there might be an alternative master plan. "And this thought," he wrote, "is a religious thought, nay I should call it *the* religious thought." With relativity, Einstein, the original cosmic slacker, was himself touching the mind of a new god, trying to wriggle through some wrinkle in time. "It is quite possible that we can do greater things than Jesus," he said.

That, finally, was Einstein's ultimate power and hold on our imagination—eternity. It would be good to touch that, too.

6 ◆ Good Dog

Sometimes I wonder whether Albert Einstein could have pondered his own spectacular afterlife on Earth, if he ever thought he might be granted a kind of immortality. It must have crossed his mind that his theories might stand the test of time. But could he ever have imagined that his brain would, too? And how strange that a man whom he only ever met once in passing, who simply took his blood and was gone, would himself become a mobile Einstein pilgrimage site, harboring two cookie jars full of Einstein's brain chunks.

Put like that, it sounds almost blasphemous. But Thomas Harvey maintains that he did what he did out of professional duty and respect for the physicist. The brain, if indeed it was meant to live on, would live through Harvey, who acted not so much as a partisan but as a protector. Which is why, at first, the pathologist moved with great care and caution when it came to the brain—and why he confounded so many others who felt him grossly underqualified for the job of studying it.

After removing it from Einstein's braincase, Harvey weighed the brain at 2.7 pounds. Then, he fastidiously fixed the tissue in paraformaldehyde solution, a process by which the brain cells are actually captured in midstream so that they appear exactly as they might in a living brain, when they're actively metabolizing. Harvey next injected the brain with sucrose to better preserve it. He made exact measurements of the frontal and parietal lobes and then photographed the brain from various aspects—black-and-whites of a deeply grooved, almost treaded, specimen. If you stare long enough at these photographs, if you blur your eyes just a bit, Einstein's brain could be an unknown moon of Jupiter or simply the Mother Egg.

Finally, Harvey dissected the brain into a total of about two hundred and forty pieces, some of which were sealed in paraffin, while others were left to float raw in formaldehyde. With the idea of making slides, Harvey solicited the help of a university lab technician named Marta Keller. Using a microtome, a device not unlike a deli slicer, she shaved some brain parts into cell-thin slivers. She then slid each slice into a saline solution, floated it onto a slide where, after drying, it was stained with cresyl dye, leaving a reddish tint. Even today, this is an exacting procedure—the brain tissue can tear, nuclei get separated and float away—which means that it's very easy to ruin a brain.

When I tracked her down all these years later in a Maine nursing home, she spoke with a thick German accent but remembered little of Harvey or the slides she made for him. "I suppose it was interesting," she said, now ninety-four and frail. When Harvey went to her, she must have been a highly competent technician, for some of those experts who've ultimately come by slides of Einstein's brain still praise her work.

Harvey also consulted with various researchers at the Wistar Institute, a University of Pennsylvania facility once famous for its vast collection of brains and bones. Founded in 1894 by Isaac Wistar, a Civil War veteran and a colorful American whose life could fill several volumes, the Wistar Institute once boasted of possessing Walt Whitman's brain, though sometime near the beginning of this century a research assistant accidentally dropped it. According to matter-of-fact newspaper accounts from the time, Whitman's brain was then tossed out in the day's garbage.

Who can say what fate awaits us?

Out of curiosity, I visit the Institute on my own months after our road trip and am given a tour by the resident librarian-historian,

Nina Long, a short, busy woman, who leads me to "the goodies" in the basement. She navigates through an obstacle course of portable silver freezers holding all kinds of germ samples, and stops before a storage closet. "It's going to be weird," she warns over her shoulder, working an old key in an old lock. "I just like to make sure people are prepared before they enter."

Inside it's dark and cramped, and when my eyes adjust to a dim bulb, I realize we're standing in a room full of mummies and skulls. There are maybe a half dozen brains floating in formaldehyde, brains of great people like Edward Drinker Cope and Joseph Leidy, the distinguished fathers of paleontology who, in the late 1800s, first discovered the dinosaur bones that proved our land once crawled with ten-story lizards. Also, there is the right arm of Isaac Wistar—one hit by a musket shot at the battle of Ball's Bluff—and then the rest of him set in jars: his scraggly aorta, his decomposing brain, and, oddly, the bones of his horse. When I see this for the first time, all of it shelved like candy-store treats, I take one step backward—right into the arms of a skeleton—and stifle a schoolgirl scream.

"That's one of our Chinamen," says Long, picking a bony finger from my shoulder. "We've got thirteen of them—full skeletons—but don't ask why, because I'm not sure."

The idea of this catacomb full of old body parts spooks me. And yet from Harvard to Cornell to UCLA, there are hundreds of such cobwebbed closets and poorly lit back rooms, such secret and not-so-secret collections of floating brains and viscera, a Gothic underworld of the suspended dead. As a kid, I was awed by the stories of Catholic believers stashing the bones of saints in underground caves because it was thought they had the emerald glow of heaven on them. But what of these human odds and ends?

Take the case of Vladimir Ilyich Lenin, one that Harvey has followed with interest. Ailing at the end of his life, he suffered several strokes, and then died in 1924, uttering the classic last words, "Good dog!" The Soviet leadership removed Lenin's brain and over the protestations of his wife, embalmed his body, dressed it in a spotted tie and period coat, and displayed it as one of the Soviet Union's most important public symbols. A popular Soviet slogan became "Lenin is more alive than all the living," and cosmonauts and newly-weds alike would visit him before embarking on their respective voyages.

Where the Catholic Church long claimed to possess Mary Magdalene's arm in Normandy or the foreskin of Christ in Italy in order to establish some direct line to heaven, Stalin did something of the same with Lenin's brain. In 1926, he founded the Moscow Brain Institute, a five-story brick building near the Yauza River in the center of the capital, in order to deconstruct the particulars of Lenin's genius. After pickling in formaldehyde for a couple of years while his comrades bickered, Lenin's brain was put to a microtome, sliced into 31,000 pieces, made into slides, and locked away in Room 19 behind a battery of metal doors, where it remains today. Over time, it has been joined by the brains of Stalin himself, Pyotr Tchaikovsky, and Andrei Sakharov.

In 1994, nearly seventy years after the study of Lenin's brain began in top secrecy, the results were released. The Institute's director, Oleg Adrianov, couldn't have been more blunt. Lenin's brain was "nothing sensational," while Stalin's brain hadn't any "special features at all." It had once been a widely held theory, one increasingly dismissed today, that the heavier the brain the more genius it contained. But Lenin's brain tipped the scales at nearly three pounds, enough in the world of celebrity brains to outweigh Anatole France's slight 2.1-pounder and Walt Whitman's 2.8-er, but then not even close to the writer Ivan Turgenev's 4.4-pound elephant. In the end, it seemed that, for many, Lenin's brain amounted to nothing more than a Maltese Falcon, a kind of terrible ruse. "It sure is a shame," says Harvey. "But we're finding the opposite with Einstein's brain."

Knowing that he didn't have the expertise to conduct a study alone, Harvey immersed himself in the medical texts of the 1950s, a pathologist reading the leading neuroanatomists, sussing out the field, considering possible candidates for collaboration. He closely studied the work of Hartwig Kuhlenbeck and scribbled penciled notes in his own meticulous hand in the margins of Percival Bailey and Gerhardt von Bonin's *The Isocortex of Man*. He came to appreciate, if not idolize, the neuroanatomists Jerzy Rose and Walle Nauta. He sent slides of Einstein's brain to a Chicago neurologist named Sidney Schulman, who today still remembers Harvey's "diffuse enthusiasm and naïveté." But then others who were sent slides at the time gave voice to what might have been Harvey's greatest fear: There was nothing at all remarkable about the specimen. Einstein's brain was just another brain.

When I think about Dr. Harvey, about the general placidity of his being, about his featureless features, about trolling the streets of Philadelphia on the first day of our road trip past these sites from a previous life, I realize that, unlike the face of a boxer or a barfly, he's someone who doesn't seem to wear his history at all. According to colleagues at Princeton Hospital, most of whom are octogenarians themselves now, Harvey's first marriage began to dissolve after Einstein's death, a mess that allegedly climaxed in Harvey's affair with a nurse at the hospital. "I remember she was a pretty, blond, buxom lass," says Dr. David Rose, a former OB-GYN who was working at Princeton Hospital in 1955. One version of the story is that Harvey's wife found out about the relationship and took the matter to the hospital director, John Kauffman. A strenuous, driven administrator, he, in turn, tried to fire his pathologist.

Unlike the modern, buttoned-up facility it is today, the Princeton Hospital of the 1950s resembled a kind of Peyton Place, according to Rose. Thus, to have fired Harvey on the grounds of an extramarital tryst would have meant firing many others on staff. And besides, says Dr. Benjamin Wright, a contemporary of Harvey's, the pathologist had done nothing in his day-to-day work to warrant Kauffman's ire. "He was a professional in every way," says Wright. The story goes that

Harvey stood up to Kauffman, claiming that if the hospital director had a desire to make Harvey's private life the issue, he would in turn make an issue of the director's private life. Kauffman immediately switched tracks and seized on Harvey's handling of Einstein's brain—the inappropriateness of how he had attained it and the years now gone by without a study.

A standoff ensued. According to Dr. Harvey Rothberg, who wrote a history of the medical center that was published in 1995, a series of meetings were called that included Harvey, Kauffman, members of the medical staff, and the trustees. The trustees decided to dismiss Harvey, but the medical staff objected and called for the immediate resignation of Kauffman. "A lot of us protested," says Wright, "we liked Harvey and thought it unfair." Finally, the trustees ousted the pathologist.

Harvey himself won't even acknowledge the episode, claiming he left the hospital of his own accord because "it was time to move on." The denial is vintage Harvey because he really believes it—and because I find myself wanting to believe it, too, as a kind of relief to that other image of a younger Harvey, in the prime of his life, disgraced and shot down, packing up and leaving his boys and first wife behind, placing Einstein's brain in the trunk of his car and driving, perhaps like we are now, into an uncertain future.

And then time passed. In the years that followed, Harvey took jobs in mental institutions and research facilities, tried to start a nursing home, did whatever he could to find interesting work. He moved west, went into family practice in Missouri, provided his medical services at Leavenworth Prison. Later, while in his seventies, he failed a three-day Kansas State medical exam, which effectively ended his career as a doctor. Meanwhile, he made and broke compacts of love, and two additional wives later, more than three decades after Einstein's death, he found himself living anonymously in Lawrence, working in a plastics factory, sleeping on the bed of a fold-out couch in a cramped apartment, staring down the end of the millennium with perhaps the millennium's greatest brain still on his shelf.

At his nadir, Harvey seems to have reapplied himself to the research of Einstein's brain. Over the course of the 1980s, he began to send out portions of the brain to about a dozen people. Those pieces ended up as far as Germany, Venezuela, China, and Japan, in the hands of not just doctors but a small, odd collection of pilgrims, too. Ever wary, Harvey is uncomfortable talking about his decision-making or the various proposals floated by entrepreneurs and venture capitalists, anatomical museums and famous people for Einstein's brain. He remains tight-lipped about whether or not there are actual plans to clone the brain—an idea that might in fact be feasible were there viable DNA to recover from any one of its 240 chunks. What he will talk about, albeit somewhat fuzzily, are concrete medical findings.

There's the work of the Japanese researcher Haruyasu Yamaguchi, who has been studying Einstein's late-in-life memory loss and the possible onset of senility by examining neurofibrillary tangles and senile plaques in the brain. In Buenos Aires, Dr. Jorge Columbo has been analyzing Einstein's cerebral cortex astroglia with mixed success. And then Dr. Charles Boyd of Australia—a seemingly good-natured man who keeps Einstein's genetic material in a container marked "Big Al's Brain"—has studied brain samples for traces of hereditary disease in the Einstein family. In addition, he has attempted to match the DNA of a skin sample provided by Evelyn Einstein with that of her grandfather's brain. Formally adopted by Hans Albert, Evelyn's paternity remains in question, and while some claim that she is in fact the illegitimate daughter of Albert himself, the test has so far proven inconclusive.

There have also been a few papers. One bears the name of both Harvey and Dr. Britt Anderson, a member of the neurology department at the University of Alabama. (According to Anderson, he did all of the research and then sent it to Harvey for a preliminary read-through before it was published.) Entitled "Alterations in Cortical Thickness and Neuronal Density in the Frontal Cortex of Albert Einstein," the short, inconclusive paper states that Einstein's cortex is thinner than those of the control brains against which he compared it—and then more densely populated with neurons (47,000 per cubic millimeter in Einstein versus 35,000 in the other brains). Anderson writes, "Could the difference in cortical packing density in any way account for Einstein's superior intellectual skills?" But then, there's no way to tell.

A second and more widely known paper is that by Dr. Marian Diamond, a neuroanatomist at the University of California at Berkeley. Diamond claims to have counted in Einstein's parietal lobe a higher than normal number of glial cells, which nourish the brain. Seventy-three percent more, to be exact. Thus, the ratio of neuronal cells to glial cells is "significantly smaller" when they were compared to those of eleven other brains and, according to Diamond, "might reflect the enhanced use of this tissue" in the expression of Einstein's "unusual conceptual powers."

Larry Kruger, a professor of neurobiology at UCLA—and a man whose postdoctoral work for Jerzy Rose gave him a front row on the earlier jockeying for Einstein's brain—says that he speaks for many in his field when he calls the "meager findings" on Einstein's brain "laughable," and remembers that when Diamond delivered her paper at a conference, the audience found the result "comical," because "it means absolutely nothing."

In the flesh, Marian Diamond is a handsome woman with an amazing white bouffant and the owner of impeccable professional credentials. Everything about her seems to glitter, like Glinda the Good Witch but with a very serious motor running between the ears. When I later tell her of Kruger's comments, she smilingly responds that he has "a lack of inhibitor cells" and says that his reaction might have had more to do with "tensions between two men"—Kruger and Diamond's husband, Arnold Scheibel, a noted brain specialist who also is on the staff at UCLA—than anything concerning her work on Einstein's brain. In response to others who have criticized her, she says, "Well, we have to start somewhere, don't we?"

Harvey, however, spins it with a little more drama. "You see," he says, "we're finding out that Einstein's brain is more unusual than many people first thought." And when it comes to the dissemination of its pieces, he paints himself as a bold leader who's carefully hand-picked an international squadron of distinguished movers and shakers after reading their work. By some of their own admissions, however, many contacted him first, then months—in some cases, years—later, received anonymous packages containing wrapped pieces of brain.

Of all those who have received parts of Einstein's brain, no one has as much—nearly one-fifth of the brain, says Harvey—as Dr. Sandra Witelson, the Canadian researcher at McMaster University in Hamilton. Witelson, a psychologist known for her gender studies, invited Harvey to visit her, and according to Harvey she organized his ephemera and articles on the brain into a scrapbook, and he turned over some portion of the brain to her.

"She's a real firecracker," says Harvey. "She has one of the biggest collections of brains around. She gets them from a local undertaker. I think her work on Einstein's brain will be quite significant." While Witelson claims that Harvey's assertions about her are "incorrect"— denies having any of Einstein's brain, then later admits that she does—some simply consider her an opportunist.

"Studying Einstein's brain [is] just a dumb idea," says Dale Purvis, a professor of neurobiology at Duke University. "One would have absolutely no idea where to look for the skills Einstein had, where his intuition and intelligence about physics came from. Presumably he was a klutz at other things, like playing basketball or balancing his checkbook. There's no reason to believe his brain is different than anybody else's."

"It's like Descartes's belief that the pineal gland is the seat of the soul," says Robert Schulman, the former director of the Einstein papers project. "[Einstein would] think it was horse shit, mythologizing without any scientific basis. He'd think it was ridiculous that people were slicing up his mind to see where his power came from."

And there are others who find the whole exercise distasteful. The first time I call Evelyn Einstein to broach the idea of a meeting with Harvey and her grandfather's brain (Harvey himself never calls her), she says, "Ah, yes, the White Rabbit." Then falls silent for a moment. "He lived in Kansas; his name's Harvey. Enough said." She's referring to the 1950 Jimmy Stewart movie entitled *Harvey* in which Stewart, who is pleasantly deranged, gets into all sorts of high jinx with an oversized, imaginary rabbit named Harvey. Then she hardens. "It's *dégoûtant*," she says. "It's disgusting what he's done." When I tell her that Harvey would very much like to see her, she is slightly taken aback, but slowly warms to mild curiosity. "I'm interested in science," she says. "I'm curious about the brain. And besides, I have to have a sense of humor about this. It's really the only way I can deal with it."

One of those with no sense of humor about it is Roger Richman, whose Los Angeles agency licenses Albert Einstein's image and represents the beneficiaries of the Einstein estate, which itself is presided over by Hebrew University. Having recently threatened legal action, he is distressed by Harvey's treatment of the brain. In attempts to project the appropriate image of Einstein—to tirelessly manicure Einstein, the Concept—there are certain things Richman forbids. For instance, he won't allow Einstein's image to be used to promote barbershops. He won't tolerate any hokey or crass besmirchments of the great genius. And the brain is his bugaboo. "If someone's writings belong to the estate and the image they've developed over their lifetime belongs to the estate, the brain must, too," says Richman, rehearsing what could eventually become the basis for a lawsuit against Harvey. "These people should be cherished, not chopped up."

7 • The Book of Us

We're up early the next morning and on the road before breakfast, stringing north of Dayton. The earth of Ohio looks pale and vulnerable, as if it's been under a winter-long Band-Aid. At a rest stop near the Indiana border, we pull off the highway, and at a bank of pay phones I call Sara, who's also been up for hours, pushing to finish her book. She tells me it's still snowing in Maine and that Trout has been hunting squirrels all morning and that the dog is now sitting on the stoop, panting, with a little party hat of snow on her snout. She tells me she herself just took some kava kava, an herb that she has recently come to believe holds mystical properties, and wonders why the federal government doesn't just dump the stuff in our water source to make the country a happier place.

I tell her that things are going fine. Harvey's holding up great and that we're fixing to see some of his old friends in Kansas when we get there. We both put the best face on our lives since we last saw each other two days ago. When she asks about the brain and I tell her it's in the trunk, she's silent for a moment, then says, "It really is, huh? It's really true?" We talk for maybe ten minutes, perfunctory talk in a way that we're never really perfunctory, all of it skirting the question of us, and I begin to wonder if she had caller ID whether she'd have picked up at all.

"Is this too weird?" I finally ask.

"Is what weird?"

"Should I not call?"

"You can call," she says softly and seems to mean it.

"You know, I just wanted to say . . . hi."

"So, it's hi then."

"Yeah, it's hi . . . and . . ."

"And?"

"I miss you out here."

"I miss you back here. . . . I just wish . . . things . . . were . . . different."

"Like . . . ?"

"Like, we can't talk about it. I mean we can't do it like this. You at a rest stop. And the book, right now. The deadline. We can't do this now."

Then there's a long silence, and even after we agree to hang up, I can't say good-bye—won't say it. I just wait for Sara to hang up. I listen to the line as it disconnects, to the last wave of electricity as it pulses from Maine to the Hoosier State, from her to me, and then wait for the thick silence that flows behind it. I stand with the phone pressed to my ear, head down, listening to that silence for a while, and then the click and crackle on the line as I'm rerouted to a recorded message: *Please hang up and try again. . . .*

Usually, when we're apart, Sara and I still find a way to talk for hours on the phone, or within the span of ten minutes somehow make it feel as if it's been hours. Early in our relationship, when we lived apart for a time, we'd talk every night on the phone, and on several occasions we babbled for so many hours in a row, I literally drifted to sleep on the sofa. Those phone calls, those million words and stories, merely became the beginning of the Book of Us. So how had we worked ourselves to this impasse? How was it that everything seemed so wrong, so suddenly . . . feelingless?

Here's what I think now: At first, you fall in love. You wake in the morning woozy and your twilight is lit with astral violet light. You spelunk down into each other until you come to possess some inner vision of each other that becomes one thing, Us Together. And time passes. Like the forming of Earth itself, volcanoes rise and spew lava. Oceans appear. Rock plates shift. Sea turtles swim half the ocean to lay eggs on the mother island; songbirds migrate over continents for berries from a tree. You evolve—cosmically and geologically. You lose each other and find each other again. Every day. Until love gathers the turtles and the birds of your world and encompasses them, too.

For miles on the interstate, I analyze the phone call, and after a time I allow my thoughts to settle—or rather allow them to be overtaken by the forward motion of our car. Eighty miles an hour, velocity becomes the measure of our progress, the speed of forgetting. Out the window, it's just so many trees and markers, fence posts and farm fields—the actual, physical, transforming thing of America itself.

We zoom across Indiana and Illinois, the two states conjoined like Siamese twins, beneath scudding clouds and clear shots of sunlight, the chill air fragrant with manure and feed. Over cold-running creeks and gullies full of old refrigerators and engine blocks, we stealth through shadows thrown by on-deck crop dusters and Greyhound buses, glance up against wobbling fifty-three-foot truck trailers full of movie videos or bananas or industrial turbines—all moving in subversive caravans—and, at one point, a flatbed with a Vietnam-era helicopter strapped to it.

In bright sun and wind appear the outbuildings and barns of the Midwest, near where Dickey-clad farmers stand in small circles eyeing their fields like nervous, hand-wringing fathers-to-be—or sometimes, merely like doomed survivors—repairing their threshers, turning the first soil, pointing to what's yet invisible, speaking in incantations: feed and fertilizer, moisture content and till depth. With each day's work, with each field-side conference and hour alone in the air-conditioned cab of a supertractor, they will silently appeal to the circadian rhythms of some higher power for a perfect calibration of sun and rain, as well as for the perfect ascension of market prices to deliver a bountiful harvest. On the radio, we get the farm report: lean hog futures down ten; feeder cattle futures up seven. Corn futures and soybean and cocoa up two and a quarter, down a half, and no change. March sugar, July corn, September rice, and December cotton—all of them attached to a momentary price that may right now be making someone rich as it bankrupts someone else.

"Look at that cow!" exclaims Harvey, bursting from his own deep silence.

Black with a white rump, it is quite a cow! On this, our third day together, something is beginning to happen out here between us—the three of us. Time is slowing, it seems, or expanding to fill a bigger sky, a more open landscape. The frantic floodlight charge of the East has given way to a single lit parlor lamp. And under it, a cow or one silver tree in the wind or the rusted remains of an old tiller seems more holy, even mythic. It's not that the Midwest lacks bustle; it's just that away from the cities, the deadlines are imposed by the earth and its seasons. I slip off my watch and feel myself beginning to slow into Harvey time.

And the land—the way America keeps coming and coming in rich, if now fallow fields, stretching to the horizon, the way the awesome power of this endlessness is the key to some deep sense of freedom—begins to reimpose an ancient language of wind and silence. It's all so strangely beautiful and at the same time raises the ghost of some kind of melancholy, a thought that, though we belong to this country as much as this country belongs to us, we only move through its rooms as momentary visitors, projecting our ideas on its walls, that the best we can do is live a good life, perhaps add a couple of replicas of ourselves, but then must hand it over, however temporarily again, to another generation—Generation Y, Generation Z . . . then what? Do we begin at A again? Or does time end when we run out of alphabet?

On these very tracks before us came the first settlers who labored to St. Louis, then set out in covered wagons across the plains facing starvation, Indians, the unknown. After them followed railroad men and prospectors and bankers and wave after wave of immigrants—all of them really only coupled by faith. Now we are long-haul truckers, retirees in RVs, job transfers in Ryders and U-Hauls, and college students—a new nation of different immigrants, searching out our plow and ten acres—whizzing along the interstate next to old wagon ruts, arriving at the Mississippi River the way they might have: ebullient, teary, praising hallelujah.

But the Mississippi isn't open for baptisms today. A momentary upriver thaw has set it loose with high water, and by the time it's made St. Louis, by the time it's been birthed from its first trickles out of Lake Itasca in northern Minnesota, picked up speed and caught the blue pulse of the St. Croix River south of St. Paul; after it's already borrowed the Rock River in Illinois, usurped Iowa's Des Moines, held up the Illinois, and sucked in the Missouri, it's one pissed and frothy mother rushing with alluvium, sturgeon, and pebbles from prehistory.

It occurs to me here, on the bridge over this very river, in the shadow of St. Louis's Gateway Arch, both magisterial and kind of puny at once, that we're retracing Harvey's footsteps when he left New Jersey, already having led a full life in his first five years with the brain. Certainly it would have occurred to him almost immediately after the autopsy that he had taken an important hostage. And certainly the once-anonymous Dr. Thomas Harvey now had to be handled with delicacy and due respect by those whose interest lay in the retrieval of Einstein's brain.

Indeed, there were many who wanted what Harvey had, including the U.S. Army, represented by one of its finest doctors, Webb Haymaker. A skinny man with protruding ears who looked a bit like Ray Bolger as the Scarecrow, Haymaker was a highly regarded neuroanatomist who, among his many credentials, had undertaken a study of Mussolini's brain. In addition, he was the author of a paper entitled "Stratomouse" in which he launched a rodent into space via high-altitude balloon in order to study the effects of radiation on the cells of living creatures. It was Haymaker who contacted Dr. Harvey just months after Einstein's death, inviting him to a summit meeting of the day's leading brain researchers in Washington, D.C. Included among the august collection were men like Harvey's hero Hartwig Kuhlenbeck, and Clem Fox, Gerhardt von Bonin, Jerzy E. Rose, and Walle Nauta.

And necessarily among them, but perhaps regarded with a tinge of condescension, this slightly awkward, nervously chuckling half doctor, this Irregular Sock, this pathologist from a small-town hospital connected only by the same name to the hallowed halls and elite eating clubs of Princeton University. According to Harvey, the meeting started with a reserved politeness, Haymaker laying out his plans for Einstein's brain, Harvey listening. But in Haymaker's patter was the presumption that the brain was already his, that Harvey would just roll over, have his belly scratched, and then Haymaker could steal his bone. When Harvey resisted, niceties flew south. Haymaker flat-out demanded the brain, Harvey simply refused. Heh-heh. When Haymaker got angry, Harvey didn't budge. When Harvey was reminded with whom he was dealing (the U.S. Army, winner of two world wars), he said, "Way-ell . . . ," and stood his ground. And now who laughs last? Who's dead, each last one of them, and who's out here busting for California with the brain, inhaling Frostys and baked potatoes, hoovering pancakes and green salads and chicken noodle soup?

"Harvey didn't know his ass from his elbow from the brain," says Larry Kruger, Jerzy Rose's postdoctoral fellow at the time. "He refused to give up the brain even though he wasn't a neuropathologist, and then all bets were off. I mean, what were you going to do with it anyway? I heard he kept it in his basement and would show it to visitors. I guess some people show off a rare edition of Shakespeare. He would say, 'Hey, wanna see Einstein's brain?' The guy's a jerk. . . . He wanted fame and nothing came of it."

When I later visit Kruger in Los Angeles, among the clutter of his UCLA office, which includes an oversized book entitled *A Dendrocyto myeloarchitectonic Atlas of the Cat's Brain*, he mentions something that I'll hear again and again, almost as a threat, or a way of reclaiming the ethical day for all slighted brain researchers in white coats with labs full of floating brains: "What Harvey did is probably illegal," he tells me. "I guess he must be a slightly strange guy. Had he been smart, he would have given it up and moved away from it, but he was grandstanding, and I presume he paid a price for it."

Even the FBI kept track of Harvey, clipping occasional articles about the pathologist and Einstein's brain, and adding them to the secret file on Einstein. If J. Edgar Hoover thought Albert Einstein was dangerous alive, it's quite possible he also found him dangerous in death. After all, the idea of Einstein's brain finding its way to the Soviet Union, to the Brain Institute, where Lenin's brain had already been sliced, diced, and secretly studied, would have been chilling in a Cold War environment where anything from a Martian invasion to a world-death machine seemed as immediately possible as the cloning of the world's greatest brain.

Once it became clear that Harvey meant to hang on to the brain, though, opinion ossified against him. And over time, the retelling of the actual autopsy became more and more gruesome, one full of horror and pagan ritual, one that was also punctuated by the removal of Einstein's eyes by Einstein's ophthalmologist, Dr. Henry Abrams, who took them because, as he tells me later, "they were part of the brain, too, and I wanted a keepsake."

In a 1994 article that ran in *The Guardian*, a British newspaper, Jonathan Freedland summed up that 1955 day like this: "At best, some sharp ethical corners were cut. At worst, the pathologist's lab was turned into a butcher's kitchen, with open season on the corpse of an old man, who happened to be one of the most significant figures in human history. (Some accounts suggest the knife-happy medical staff did not stop at the eyes and brain: One contemporary recalls seeing Einstein's heart and intestines the next day, in a 'bucket.') As Abrams admits, in the excitement of handling the body of a legend, 'Nobody gave any thought to anything.' "

And though Harvey is the Sweeney Todd of this Boschian vision, the same article describes Harvey today as "a harmless old buffer, with a rasping laugh." Others have been less generous. In a poem entitled "Love Letter, Static Interference from Einstein's Brain," the writer Joyce Carol Oates picks up on the legend of her Princeton hometown, claiming that what Harvey did was "wicked." Near the end of his life, Otto Nathan made it clear that Harvey had acted against the wishes of the Einstein estate, giving rise to the popular, apparently sanctioned version of Harvey as a heretic let loose in the temple. For many years, when Harvey's old teacher Harry Zimmerman was asked about Harvey's whereabouts, he claimed, out of ignorance or desire, that his student was dead.

It's from Harvey's lost decades with the brain that his myth has grown to weird pop-cult status, attracting odd notices in odd places. In a 1978 issue of *New Jersey Monthly* a writer, Steven Levy, tracked him to Kansas where, according to Levy, Harvey kept the brain stashed behind a beer cooler in a box marked Costa Cider. And, nearly twenty years later, a heavy-metal quartet known as Attic of Love chronicled the dreams of a stoner plotting his own theft of Einstein's brain from Harvey in the song "Stealing Einstein's Brain":

> *He heard the rumor one morning; somewhere out in the*
> * Midwest*
> *Einstein's brain was adorning a trophy shelf by the desk*
> *of a general practitioner gentleman. Who was he to be so blessed?*
> *So he formed a plan to take a stand,*
> *and one day he'd attain the theft of Einstein's brain.*
> *Stealing Einstein's brain.*

And then, in 1993, a British filmmaker named Kevin Hull visited Harvey in Lawrence while making his own documentary about the brain. The result, *Einstein's Brain*, is so wackily good that I decide to visit Hull in London, before hitting the road with Harvey, in order to get a second opinion on the old man. When I arrived, the whole of England seemed bawling and busted open, lost in its own apocalypse of Christmas parties turned to drunken sadness in the gutter of Covent Garden. In a little bistro, over spinach salad, sausage, and cod, I talked with Hull about everything from the fate of the world to the difference between British and American urinals. He confided that, on a tip from the MI6 during the filming of his latest documentary on the British defense industry, he had information that Japan is now building its own weapon of mass destruction under Los Alamos–type secrecy.

Apropos of nothing but my fourth glass of wine, I felt compelled to return his confidence with a bizarre dream from the night before, one in which I found myself lost in a strange land, beset by stones thrown by a hungry, cynical crowd of zealots, something out of Shirley Jackson's "The Lottery," but then I wouldn't fall down, wouldn't give up some little nugget of myself that they seemed to want. No, in fact, the more rocks I took to the body, the more exhilarated I began to feel.

Hull listened closely with a perplexed expression, thick brows knitted like two caterpillars, then he leaned forward, suddenly cutting through the haze of my merlot meanderings, fixing me with beady, intense eyes, and said with equal apropos, as if the two are related: "Harvey pinched it. The bloke bloody pinched it. . . ."

"Pinched what?"

"The brain."

"You mean, he stole it?"

"Couldn't be more black and white," he said. "There are a couple of things you won't find. First, a record of the autopsy. It's missing. Second, the letter from Hans Albert to Harvey bequeathing the brain to him."

"There was such a letter?"

"Exactly my point. As far as we know, no one bequeathed Harvey the brain."

But then when I ask Harvey point-blank if he stole the brain, he bristles, standing by his version of events: Nathan authorized him to remove the brain, and Hans Albert authorized him to study it. On the matter of Abrams and Einstein's eyes, Harvey frowns, then turns uncharacteristically angry. "I didn't agree with what he did at all," he snaps. "He got in touch a few years ago and offered me the eyes, but I didn't want them. What was I going to do with them?"

Abrams, on the other hand, tells me that, but for the exchange of an occasional holiday card, he hasn't had any contact with Harvey since Harvey left Princeton Hospital nearly four decades ago, un-equivocally denying that he ever offered Harvey the eyes. He says that now, once or twice a year, when he opens the safe-deposit box in a Philadelphia vault where he keeps Einstein's eyes, when he gazes upon two white planets, each set with the most remarkable orb of brown, he's filled with warm memories and "a deep connection" to the pro-fessor. And then, too, he denies rumors that he may be in negotiations with Michael Jackson, the pop star-cum-collector of body parts, to sell the eyes for a price rumored to be several million dollars.

Gregory Stock, a professor at UCLA and the author of *Metaman: The Merging of Humans and Machines into a Global Superorganism*, feels that any mention of a market price on Einstein's eyes or brain could only serve to drive Harvey deeper into the shadows. An ac-quaintance of one of Harvey's sons, Stock pitched Harvey on a pro-posal to rebuild the brain, piece by piece—to create a 3-D reconstruction with the idea that the brain would then go on tour. Stock claims he wasn't thinking about turning Einstein's brain into a money-making venture, but Harvey, who rejected the idea, claims he was. What both do agree on, however, is that Stock visited Harvey in Kansas, where, according to Stock, the White Rabbit "spread the brain out on a cheese board." Like hors d'oeuvres.

Whatever Stock's own intentions, he is not the first to imagine a profitable way to deploy Einstein's brain. According to Harvey, money offers for the brain have been made by an anatomical society in Edinburgh, Scotland; the Milken Foundation in California, founded by the convicted junk-bond dealer Michael Milken; and a man claiming he desired the brain for his own personal "Museum of Historical Relics, Oddities, and Eccentricities" and who offered Harvey fifteen thousand dollars for a single piece. In addition, one entrepreneur had the idea of embedding fine slices of the brain in pens and commemorative plaques.

Beyond the simply monetary, Harvey has entertained hundreds of other requests—ranging from the belligerent to the sweetly flattering, and not all of them from the most stable of people, either. In his basement office at Cleora's house, he keeps a couple shoe boxes full of letters: A rabbi, pointing out the sacrilege of Harvey's act, demanding the brain for proper burial. The bothered words of one St. Paul woman who concludes: "The Mind comes into the brain at birth and leaves at death. . . . As I see it, you're wasting your time studying the brain. The thinking genius part has long departed. Think it over." Then there are more missives from sweet schoolkids, amateur mathematicians, huffy cranks, and a teacher from Oregon accused of sexual abuse in a case of recovered memory, pleading for cash from Harvey for his defense fund.

But has Harvey paid a price for possessing the brain, as Kruger suggests? Perhaps. He went from being a doctor to an extruder operator at a plastics factory, from being once married to thrice divorced, from somewhat comfortable circumstances to days spent in a basement. All of it after the brain, perhaps because of the brain.

"In retrospect, I think Harvey's own motivations are odd," says Stock. "In a way, that brain is his entire identity."

Nonetheless, a life isn't one paragraph long, and we might also consider Harvey a happy man, with each move maybe feeling himself on to the next adventure, with each wife and child perhaps feeling himself loved. And then look at him, tracing his finger over the map as we hovercraft into Missouri: He seems as gentle as a lamb. Still, I try to picture him standing before Einstein's body—in that one, naked moment. Did he realize then that his life would become a trail of broken commitments?

Only occasionally can you glimpse through the embrasures of an otherwise perfectly polite person to see the cannons aimed out, only in a certain glint of light do the eyeteeth become fangs. We are driven by desire and fear. Only in our solitary hungers do we find ourselves capable of the most magnificently unexpected sins.

8 ◆ How to Make Love to
the Same Person for the Rest of Your Life

We make quite a pair, Harvey and I do. Even if we are more than a half century apart in age, he born under the star of William Howard Taft and I under the napalm bomb of Lyndon Baines Johnson, if he wears black, size-seven Wallabees with purple socks and I sport space-age sunglasses and a tuft of chin hair, if he has his gaggle of ex-wives, ten children and step-children and twelve grandchildren and I have yet to procreate, we begin to think together, to make unconscious team decisions. We both drink from bottles of seltzer, a hedge, says Harvey, against "GI upset." We read the same billboards and register the same passing drivers—a man in a turban, driving a Lincoln Town Car, smoking a cigarette like a mobster; a kid who looks fourteen driving a beat-up hearse. And the most important common denominator of all, we eat the same food. A deluxe omelette at Perkins, a Frosty at Wendy's. And every time we do the drive-through at McDonald's, angling for a Coke and small fries to keep us for the afternoon, I feel like screaming: *We have Einstein's brain in the trunk!*

But who would believe me?

Even now there are doctors who claim that in our lifetimes we will see the first brain transplant or that cloning will become an everyday occurrence. In essence, they predict that science, not religion, will guarantee us an afterlife. And yet I can't help but wonder what Einstein would make of America if he sat in the backseat now—or, perhaps, what he will make of it when he sits in the backseat again.

And I wonder if this kind of afterlife would be so great after all. Einstein's brain in the body of Fabio? Or Einstein regenerated, living a life on top of the life he's already led, doomed by the accomplishments of his former self. A life already confined, categorized, and collated before it's even begun again. What would it feel like to be born with an FBI file already open on you? Or to know you had once revolutionized the world with your work, but then never found true love? Might you try to trade one for the other? Or would you just sit around smoking pot all day, rebelling against yourself?

On the one hand, of course, Einstein would be horrified by our world and its extravagances: the Land of the Free and the Home of the SUVs. The absurdities of our Whopper-sized lives. And perhaps, too, he'd be stunned by the sheer roaring speed and interconnectedness of it. He'd have no shortage of complaints: MTV, Microsoft, the fast-food neon oasis-pods of the interstate—all of them ballpeening the masses into one lump of hip-hop, mouse-click conformity. He'd be shocked by his own Q rating, the fact that, in the time that has passed since his death, he's perhaps even more well-known than he was alive. A poster boy for the new millennium. And yet there would be so many bemusing, baffling things ripe for Einstein's sharp sense of humor: tae-bo and tofu burgers, Jesse Ventura and Bill Clinton, silicone breasts and penis augmentations.

Simply having Einstein's brain in the trunk rearranges the way you see everything. And then, here in the Skylark, a kind of natural selection has occurred: The atlas, with Harvey's speckled hand atop, occupies the most prime real estate between us, as do the M&M's and Stoned Wheat Thins. Scattered in this region, too, are a few of my road go-tos, my ur-tapes—good for any predicament, from sleepiness to road rage. On the backseat are some of my books. This is a habit of mine, to bring along monster tomes like *Moby Dick* or *Ulysses* or *Remembrance of Things Past*—as a kind of security should we, say, break down in the panhandle of Texas for three or four weeks—but then never so much as crack one of them. In the back

well we continue to deposit our newspapers and trash, watch it pile
with quiet satisfaction.

Harvey and I possess our own talismans, too. In Harvey's case, it's
the green beret, which he sets on his knee, or works along its rim with
busy fingers like a string of prayer beads. Meanwhile, I've propped
Thurman Munson's 1979 baseball card on the dash, one that I have a
habit of carrying around, a photo of the Yankee captain with his wal-
rus mustache and slightly ridiculous sideburns. Munson wasn't
good-looking in the traditional sense—maybe not in *any* sense—but
he was the junkyard heart and soul of those great late-seventies
Yankee teams and he played through his injuries, willing himself
onto the field with stitched-up gashes and staph infections, swollen
knees and inflamed shoulders. And he was my man.

I've often wondered why a skinny, nine- or ten- or eleven-year-old
twerp would identify with a gruff, brawling grown man who once
poured a plate of spaghetti on a reporter's head. What shred of same-
ness could exist between a do-gooding altar boy and a foulmouthed,
truck driver's son who threw bats at cameramen? But then I was a
catcher, too. In my town's Little League, I'd suit up in oversized pads
and move as if I were carrying a pack of rocks on my back. Just playing Thurman Munson's position bestowed some of his magic on me.
Each wild pitch taken to the body, each bruise and jammed finger,
was in honor of the ones taken by Thurman Munson, pain connecting two human beings on a level that went beneath intellect and experience and age. In my mind, we were the same dog.

And then, for my brothers and me, his death was our Kennedy as-
sassination. Practicing takeoffs and landings in Canton, Ohio, between games, Munson mistakenly put his Cessna into a stall. Just
before the runway, the plane dipped precipitously, scraped trees, tum-
bled down toward a cornfield, hit the ground at 108 miles per hour,
spun, and had its wings shorn off. There were two other passengers on
board who survived and they tried to drag Thurman Munson from
the wreckage. He was conscious, probably paralyzed, calling for help.

And all of a sudden jet fuel leaked, pooling near him, and the Cessna exploded. Afterward, he was identified by dental records. "The body is that of a well developed, well nourished, white male," read the autopsy, "who has been subjected to considerable heat and fire, which has resulted in his body assuming the pugilistic attitude." When someone retrieved his car, his Mercedes 450SL convertible, later that day, there was still a cigar lit and smoking in the ashtray.

Harvey doesn't know a thing about Thurman Munson. He tells me about a Yale scatback from 1931 by the name of Albie "The Mighty Atom" Booth, a small, tricky runner who single-handedly buried teams with end zone to end zone kick returns, power sweeps that sent him slingshotting through the defense, and an accurate foot that beat Harvard 3 to 0 in his last game ever. "Boy, could he run!" Harvey says, and in my mind I conjure an image of Harvey in Ivy regalia, fur coat and Eli banner cheering Albie Booth, though I know it probably never was.

On this our third day together, the February sun keeps circling our car as we roll through Missouri. And now there's a bird following us—a big black crow. I take it as a sign. But of what?

Maybe it's something about the day, or the fact that we're gobbling up the miles to Kansas City, where Harvey has kin, but Harvey is stuck on telling random tales of this country's history. He begins each with words like: "In the days of canals . . ." or "I remember the Depression for its coffee. . . ." He tells me about the Dalton Gang, a bunch of brothers and their friends from Kansas who went from law-abiding to bank-robbing for no apparent reason and had an auspicious run across the plains, terrorizing everyone, until a couple of the brothers got shot. Often they would hit a bank or a train and then lay low for a while in the town of Meade, Kansas. Harvey tells me what he knows about the boys, but in a slow-motion way that leaves miles of opportunity for other subjects. Which is when I try to bring up the brain one more time. Whether it's Harvey's hearing or just plain obstinance, our exchanges come out like an experimental renga:

The Dalton boys, they'd divvy the loot, heh-heh . . .
But then as impossible as it seems to believe . . .
Drunk and playing cards in their hideout, I guess . . .
You just took two jars and walked out . . .
Like these real American outlaws from Meade.

And later, when Harvey recalls a memory, this:

Knew a fella once, built sailboats, heh-heh . . .
But then why so much controversy when . . .
He built a schooner and sailed it home to Britain . . .
No one was hurt, and you say it wasn't stolen . . .
Don't know how he did it . . . and don't know why, either.

In Independence, Missouri, we break off the interstate to visit the home and presidential library of Harry S. Truman. The former owner of a haberdashery shop—and not a very successful one at that—Truman presided over some of the most significant events of our century, most of them during the first four months of his presidency: the German surrender, V-E Day, the Potsdam Conference, the formation of the United Nations, the dropping of two atomic bombs on Hiroshima and Nagasaki, the Japanese surrender. We tour the library with its various displays highlighting each gut-wrenching decision Truman had to make, and then, in Truman's office, standing before his empty desk, we hear his crisp-edged voice from a scratchy recording, emanating from invisible speakers somewhere, greeting us from the dead.

"This is Harry S. Truman speaking," says Harry Truman. "This room is an exact reproduction of the Presidential Office in the West Wing of the White House as it was in the 1950s."

Where each newspaper clipping or old photo is connected to a real time and to real people for Harvey—and where that memory opens a door to whatever feelings of patriotism or Nazi paranoia or gladness for being alive that he might have felt during the war, my attempt to imagine those days is more like that of a spectator in the upper deck. I see a lot of short people playing on a field far away: Take Truman, Hitler, Hirohito, and Churchill, combine their heights, and you have an NBA player. And yet they destroyed much of Europe and Japan, and left millions dead. Then a whole generation of Americans was spontaneously called away to fight. One day you were home working the fields and factories, working as a clerk or car salesman, and the next you were marching through France. For someone whose own generation came closest to war in a theater watching *Apocalypse Now*, it's difficult for me to make the leap, to fathom that every ideal and principle of being American could ever be placed at risk. In those years, even Harvey, a committed Quaker pacifist, went to work in a government facility, testing chemicals for weapons.

In the gift shop, I buy a handful of Roosevelt/Truman election pins and stick one to the front pocket of my hunting jacket. Leaving, we pass a middle-aged man, who, after spotting the button, shakes his head angrily and speaks loudly to his companion, another middle-aged man. "He killed more people with the stroke of a pen. I guess you could say that about him," he says. Harvey, who doesn't seem to hear the comment, turns to me and says right back, "I met Harry Truman once. It was through Cleora. She was a family friend of the Trumans and we met him here at the library before he died. We had some lemonade together. Real nice man. Down-to-earth. And a good president, too."

I can't tell if Harvey's putting me on, but then, of course he's not. He's Zelig, a character whose life somehow keeps intersecting with these other, larger lives, playing out on a canvas that encompasses all of history, which, in the end, is really the only thing that makes him compelling. Or does it? Without Einstein's brain would Harvey really just be a harmless old buffer?

Back on the interstate, Kansas City appears emerald at sunset. Shots of light glance off the glass windows of skyscrapers, electrons and quanta firing past us like an invisible hail of bullets. Everyone heading west squints and hides behind visors, eases off the accelerator just a bit, the stanching power of sunlight. Harvey closes his eyes and soaks up the warmth as if he were on a Caribbean island. He has intimated that we will be having dinner with a friend tonight, though he has refused to elaborate, and soon he is giving me directions into town until we're flowing with traffic along an avenue of strip malls to Eighth Street.

He refers to her as the "ex." The third wife, Raye. After the first ex, Ellouise, who gave him three sons, and the second ex, Alison, "a smart Australian girl," who had a sharp financial mind. This is Raye, the one who walked out on him in 1982. Large, windshield glasses that magnify her hazel eyes, thin lips, a silver mane of shoulder-length hair. A handsome beauty, an ironic smile suppressing a murky, rising sadness. A slightly disjointed gaze—halfway here, halfway to nowhere. She's sixty-five years old, has run out of money, and has moved in with her daughter, Harvey's stepdaughter Virginia. She wears a pink plastic hospital band around her wrist.

We arrive at her daughter's house, one half of a chalet-style duplex where Virginia lives with her Iranian husband and two daughters. Dr. Harvey doesn't call ahead, just shows up unannounced and they— Raye, Virginia, and the two grandkids—both brooding, dark-haired girls who seem about ten and six—act unfazed, almost as if they've been expecting him, as if he ran out for a quart of milk, even though he hasn't lived in these parts for nearly a year. "Hug Grandpa," says Virginia flatly. The littlest girl makes faces at me, sticks out her tongue, gives me the finger. I volley with a pout—*where's the love?* She wiggles her butt defiantly, points at it—like, *kiss my ass, soldier-boy*—then jumps back on the couch next to her sister, the two of them immediately glazed over by the dulcet light of the television. Harvey, trying to incite interest, glances at the screen. On the news, a clip of archetypal sitcom dad Bill Cosby, doing a standup show that evening in Kansas City.

"Hey, where's Cosby?!" Harvey says, suddenly vaudevillian. The two girls swivel their heads from the set to their grandfather, seem baffled by the disturbance, glower, then swivel back to watching. Harvey stands slumped in the middle of the room with his green beret on his fingertips, working it in busy circles.

"Tom, the least you could do is give me a hand," says Raye. She's on the other side of the room, breaking down boxes after having moved the last of her items from her old house to this one. She seems fragile, looks as if she's been crying. Harvey chuckles, clears his throat. "Sure," he says. "I'd be happy." He puts his beret on a table and awkwardly wrestles with a box as Raye neatly folds three more.

What's weird here isn't the chilly reception or the seeming lack of intimacy—they could almost all be strangers—no, I understand how people can fall apart. Rather, it's this flash moment in which I glimpse a picture of myself in Harvey. He's an old man, and alone. And here I am, in a roomful of strangers, alone too—and getting older by the second. By the time we reach San Francisco, I suspect I'll be gray and hunched myself.

Now, witnessing Harvey rendered somewhat useless, I wonder how it is that you become a man with ex-wives and ex-families, how you start as a young doctor with all the promise in the world and end up working in a plastics factory. And how you wake up near the end of that life in a body that betrays the will of your mind, rusted by rickety joints that walk you down the hall three times slower than they once did. Until you somehow find yourself standing in a generic Kansas City living room with a religious calendar on the wall, with half of America behind you and another half to go, doing mortal battle with a cardboard box, as if it's some wild alligator.

And another thing. Beneath the neutrality of the kin in this room, what I'm picking up, too, is a whiff of disapproval: Harvey, the free-wheeling, come-and-go libertine, perhaps having rolled in and out of this particular truck stop once too often on his way somewhere else. I get the feeling that perhaps the brain has been used as an excuse for more than just a road trip in his life, has pried Harvey from some of the people closest to him, employed as both weapon and defense.

As evidence, Virginia simply seems to ice him out. In Raye, it's rather a bemused frustration that masks something deeper. For between them, ex-husband and wife, some unspoken body of love has been laid to rest, and they stand awkwardly next to it now, regarding it in its coffin. Watching them delicately negotiate each other, I recall an intimation of Einstein's life in Harvey's. "I am truly a lone traveler," said the physicist near the end of his life, "and have never belonged to my country, my home, my friends, or even my immediate family with my whole heart. . . . I have never lost a sense of distance and a need for solitude."

But certainly between Harvey and Raye, as it had been between Einstein and Mileva, there must have been a day when they were first nervous in each other's presence, when they felt the ferocity of some huge, nameless thing: rapture of some kind. There must have been a feeling of shared conspiracy and all of time stretching out before them. So how does a feeling like that just evaporate?

We go to eat at Bennigan's, the three of us—Harvey, Raye, and I— and as we pass into the restaurant's kitschy old-Chicago-themed chambers, into the faux-Tiffany lamp-glow realm of microwaved meals and soda pop refills, he pulls me aside, lowers his voice so Raye can't hear, and says, "I'm paying for this one." Everything inside is friendly and brightly colored and buoys the soul. Once seated in a booth, Harvey urges Raye to order shrimp. "You love shrimp," he says. She says the last time they were out together like this she was food-poisoned by shrimp. "Remember?" He looks distractedly at a picture over her shoulder, a man with a handlebar mustache and bowler.

"What?" says Raye, tilting her head. "Is it my hair? Or something else?"

"No," says Harvey. "It's just that fella has such a funny mustache."

Before our food arrives—shrimp scampi for Harvey, soup for

Raye, a quesadilla for me—I ask Raye if she felt a degree of responsibility having Einstein's brain around the house, if living with the brain somehow changed their life together. "Oh, yes," she says, taking a deep breath as if she has much to say about the matter, "but really Tom wasn't doing anything with it. . . ."

Before she can continue, Harvey suddenly jumps in. "I know I didn't handle it well," he blurts out, vexed. "I made some mistakes." Then he abruptly changes the subject, commandeers the conversation by force, and again tells the story of the Dalton Gang—the robbing of banks, the final shootout in Meade. He takes his time telling it as if he's working against the clock, defusing some kind of bomb.

As we eat, as Harvey drones on and Raye submits to his droning, the dramas of the restaurant—the raucous guffaws of a nearby carnivore who wears his cloth napkin like an ascot, the secret whispers of a seemingly illicit meeting taking place in the booth behind ours—fall away. Until it's just Raye with her jangled heart and Harvey whose new animation hides a distracted rheumy distance. The come-close, stay-away conundrum of two people who passed through each other on their way elsewhere.

When dinner is over, we take Raye back to her daughter's house. Harvey escorts her to the door, while I stay put at the wheel. It's ten o'clock and starting to rain, a cold, insistent drizzle. Harvey and Raye share a moment on the doorstep. I watch their shadows in the light for a moment—Harvey bent a little and Raye stiff and standing apart—and then stop watching. I mess with the radio dial until I find more hog prices. And then Harvey is crab-walking back to the mother ship, falls in with a sigh of good-bye relief. Later, hundreds of miles from here, he'll realize he's misplaced his green beret, left perhaps on the table in the living room. But now we buckle and ease back out of the driveway, accelerate and vanish, jetting beneath the flare of streetlights, unspooling across the country again. Harvey and I and Einstein's brain, in the ashram of the Skylark, counting the beads of our memory, our losses and gains.

9 • Shooting the Z

Even Einstein himself couldn't have predicted what would happen to him in 1905. Prior to that year, he'd published a handful of interesting, albeit unremarkable, papers. Then, in a sudden rush, came three stunning treatises: "On a Heuristic Point of View Concerning the Production and Transformation of Light," which detailed how electromagnetic radiation interacts with matter in a way that became known as the photoelectric effect; "On the Movement of Small Particles Suspended in Stationary Liquids Required by the Molecular-Kinetic Theory of Heat," in which Einstein explored Brownian motion, validating the molecular-kinetic theory of heat; and finally, the coup de grâce, "On the Electrodynamics of Moving Bodies," which for the first time posited the special theory of relativity and was followed two months later by a short paper supposing that all energy has mass, an idea so radical that it took Einstein two years to reformulate the equation as $E=mc^2$.

Without the world knowing it yet—let alone the day's leading scientists—Einstein had single-handedly bombed the sacred hall of science, took a sledge to Newton, created a new language for understanding a new universe that seemed intricately and irretrievably different from the one humankind supposed for itself. It was all encoded in arcane equations and seemingly random flights of thought, tangled in scientific jargon that by bit seemed illogical, but added up to something hypercoherent and mind-bending.

The truth is it's almost impossible to overestimate the impact and ripple effects of relativity, which one British newspaper triumphantly called "an affront to common sense." And remarkably, where Sir Isaac Newton had fled Cambridge in 1666 during a plague and toiled alone on the law of universal gravitation at his home in the quiet English village of Woolsthorpe, Einstein scribbled the equations of relativity on scrips and scraps in his own cloister at the Patent Office. Years later, when asked by reporters to explain the theory, Einstein jokingly summed it up like this: "An hour sitting with a pretty girl on a park bench passes like a minute, but a minute sitting on a hot stove seems like an hour."

One of the most familiar examples of Einstein's special relativity goes like this: A woman is riding on a train. Seated and facing forward, she believes everything, including the lightbulb over her head, is stationary, while everything outside of the train is moving. Meanwhile, a man standing on the platform as the train passes believes everything inside the train is moving, all at the speed of the train's progress. If the woman on the train were to time a light beam as it emanates from the bulb above her head to the floor and back again to the ceiling in a straight line, the man on the platform outside would time the same light beam as it appears to move diagonally through the car. If the speed of light is constant, and the diagonal light takes longer to move from the ceiling to the floor and back again because it covers a greater distance, then the same event measured from the platform takes longer.

Which means, among other things, time is relative. Or two different sensibilities of time belong to the woman and man: a now and a then.

In addition, the train, as viewed by the man on the platform, appears to shrink in the direction it is headed. If the train were to approach the speed of light, says Einstein, the train's length would approach zero and time would stand still.

What Einstein was proposing by this thought experiment was the revolutionary idea of a relativistic universe, one no longer governed by an autonomy of laws, but a place where space and time become one thing: space time, the invisible Mylar fabric of the new cosmos. In attempts to extend this concept to encompass all of physics, and most particularly gravitation, Einstein then went to work on what, in 1916, would become the general theory of relativity. Reinventing Newton's theory of universal gravitation, Einstein imagines that a person in a box, or, say, a spaceship, hurtling toward Neptune, will be forced to the floor, though gravity has no effect in space. Similarly, an earthbound person in an elevator cut loose of its cable won't actually touch the floor of the elevator as it speeds toward the ground, as the same person in a falling elevator, placed this time in gravity-less space, won't touch the floor, either. Einstein claims that gravity has no effect on either scenario, whether it takes place on Earth or Neptune. Which means that, in each instance, acceleration creates the same effect as gravity.

Once that premise is set, Einstein extrapolates wildly, and among the many complicated ideas of the theory, general relativity supposes that the presence of a gravitational field causes space-time to be curved and so there are warps in the fabric of space-time, points near stars, planets, and moons where light beams—what Einstein calls quanta—bend. Thus comes one of the huge revelations: Matter and energy drive the bending of space-time. To verify it, and almost as a triumphant toss-off, he produces an equation predicting the exact shift of sunlight as it passes Mercury—approximately forty-three seconds of arc per century, says Einstein—the very equation that, to the astonishment of the world, Arthur Eddington confirms as correct after observing the 1919 eclipse in western Africa. While the special theory proves that time is relative, based on the absolute speed of light, the general theory proves that not only acceleration, but of all things, the speed of light, is now relative, too.

The sum and implication of these findings, however, were met with silence. Einstein had hit as many home runs as Mark McGwire,

as many RBIs as Hack Wilson, as .400 as Ty Cobb, in as many con-
secutive games as Joe DiMaggio, and had thrown in a Gold Glove
for good measure—all in one season. And at first, no one cheered.
His special theory of relativity, which he submitted as his doctoral
thesis to the Swiss Federal Polytechnical, was deemed unintelligible
and rejected. Meanwhile, the equation $E=mc^2$ could not be confirmed until the 1930s, under complicated laboratory conditions.
Even his 1921 Nobel prize wasn't awarded for relativity, which
became the source of heated debate and thus scared off the conservative Nobel committee, but rather for his work on the photoelectric effect.

Nearly a hundred years after Einstein's *annus mirabilis*, we now of
course appreciate his genius because, for most of us, Einstein has
been imprinted on us as a genius. And because his work lives on
today—in bombs and laser beams, fusion machines and the space
program. At Sandia Labs in Albuquerque, New Mexico, researchers
have made enormous strides in attempts to achieve nuclear fusion
from a small amount of electricity that would otherwise light about
forty houses. The electricity is stored and then shot into a complex of
holding tanks, a massive thing known as the Z Machine, which is
housed in a huge warehouse on the outskirts of Kirtland Air Force
Base. In one microburst—what's called "shooting the Z"—the machine has produced forty times the world's energy output, literally
lifting the warehouse off the ground. When I think of Einstein's
brain, I can't help but think of the Z Machine as its living em-
bodiment.

But Einstein never held himself quite so dear as did those around
him. Despite the demands of fame, he kept working. Days and nights
passed as if a minute had, and then, when he stood up from his visions, he was dizzy—and exhausted. In 1928, maniacally working in
pursuit of a unified field theory in which both gravitation and electromagnetism could be explained as inextricably linked phenomena,
he was hospitalized with an enlarged heart caused by overexertion.

When Helen Dukas, the woman who would soon become his secretary, met him for the first time prone in bed, he said, "Here lies an old child cadaver."

Unfortunately, he was right in more ways than one. After Einstein's last groundbreaking discovery, in 1925—the Bose–Einstein condensation phenomenon in which he, along with S. N. Bose, an Indian physicist, helped establish quantum statistics—there was a distinct feeling among Einstein's fellows that if he'd gone fishing for the last thirty years of his life it wouldn't really have mattered. Which is to say that, scientifically speaking, Einstein was pretty much finished at forty-six—roughly Harvey's age when he was fired from Princeton Hospital. But then, what about the Sisyphian effort of those remaining years, the maddening cul-de-sacs and thousands and thousands of pages and scraps and napkins scrawled with numbers, a huge, hurtling train of thought, cross-referenced and noted to one's self, that even today few people can decipher? Could it be that somewhere in Einstein's three decades of scribbled hieroglyphics, in the vault of his writings kept today at Hebrew University in Jerusalem, is a unified theory of everything?

Probably not. For even as we remember him for being a genius, he spent many more years of his life striving, foundering, confused. And while few question the wild streak of his brilliance—Einstein alone, it seems, held the seashell of the century to his ear—he still collaborated frequently, soliciting help with his math, trying unformed ideas on his colleagues until they crystallized. As he grew older, however, he became more isolated. His wives died: Elsa in 1936 and Mileva in 1948. He rarely saw his sons, and in truth, did little to repair his most intimate relationships.

In his work, it's possible that his own legend now kept him from those earlier fruitful collaborations. And where he once had attacked a problem by visualization, by drawing some simple observation from the natural world and then raising it to its abstraction, he more and more began with an abstraction and worked backward, which often merely left him wading in more abstraction. His fame didn't help matters, for his failures were often anticipated as victories. In 1929, when he published a paper attempting to explicate his unified field theory, a hundred journalists waited on his doorstep. Upon the paper's publication, a London department store posted it in the window to the crush of huge crowds. The public hoo-ha was so great that Einstein was forced into hiding even as his findings quailed under the scrutiny of colleagues.

In this way, fame was confusing. After relativity had been confirmed and Einstein had been crowned a new messiah, there'd been a kind of gold rush to possess him. And after years of toiling in obscurity, Einstein seemed to welcome the attention. At the very least, he accepted the invitations, made the trips, charmed his hosts, flirted with pretty women, lectured on relativity, attended the dinner parties, and sometimes departed without ever once changing his clothes. It wasn't so bad to be embraced by his fellow physicists— and then the world beyond. And because Einstein was extremely generous in lending his name to whatever cause suited his left-leaning sensibilities, he was always lending his name to one political cause or another. According to his FBI file, he put his signature to over seventy in all.

Along the way, too, the gate to some upper echelon of society opened and so the famous clamored for introductions. He met Sigmund Freud and Thomas Mann, Franz Kafka and Rabindranath Tagore, the Indian mystic. In letters he shared pacifist sympathies with Gandhi. He supped with his friend Charlie Chaplin and the publishing tycoon William Randolph Hearst, making the strenuous argument that the rich in America were too rich, and the poor too poor. He became fast friends with the queen of Belgium, corresponding with her regularly when he took up residence in Princeton. Much of his appeal emanated from his aura. If the first half of the 1900s are sepia photographs to us now, we must imagine Einstein as a strange, rainbow-colored creature among the black-and-white, one who seemed like a holy man. "Einstein was prone to talk about God so often," said his friend, the writer Friedrich Durrenmatt, "that I was led to suspect he was a closet theologian."

During the years when he couldn't scrounge a teaching job let alone put food on the table for his family, he'd learned the virtues of being mule-headed. Now when it came time to turn back to his work again, amid the madness surrounding him, he stubbornly shut everyone out, followed the rails of his own mind back to some horizon of inquiry at the edge of the cosmos, and fell into deep contemplation. It might have been that very stubbornness, and that lonely journeying, that became his undoing.

After Einstein's breathtaking revelations, science moved very quickly. Physicists like Niels Bohr, Max Born, Werner Heisenberg, and Erwin Schrödinger, among a score of others, penetrated what had long been terra incognita. And while most of the physicists of the day took an important right-hand turn at quantum mechanics, a theory that predicted strobe-light chaos when the universe was parsed on an atomical level, Einstein took a left. In many ways he was the same lost-in-thought man who had once shown up to work at the Patent Office in green slippers trimmed with flowers, but he'd suddenly been ejected from whatever mystical slipstream had borne him along for twenty years and was left treading water in an eddy.

"I have thought a hundred times as much about the quantum problems as I have about the general relativity theory," he said in a suggestion of defeat near the end of his life.

Even now, we really can't imagine Einstein in the dark for the last thirty years of his life, so firmly have we fit him into our definition of genius, so completely does his name alone transport us beyond ourselves to the highest realms of cogitation. But then why should Einstein be so doomed?

No, I'd rather conjure him as flesh and bones, an amiable, slightly eccentric man with a thick German accent who looks as if he's just stuck his finger in an electric socket, traveling in the early 1930s by cross-country train on a visit to Los Angeles—passing through Pennsylvania and Ohio to Chicago; from Chicago down to St. Louis, toward Kansas City, and then south to Lamy, New Mexico, out across reservation land and Arizona into southern California.

I picture a man, a perpetual foreigner seemingly at home anywhere in the cosmos, looking out at all of that American landscape, bemused and bewildered, asking questions: Why is it that, while traveling at 80 miles per hour in a locomotive, on the face of an Earth moving at 72,000 miles per hour around the sun, it feels as if we're really crawling? Or not moving at all? Why is it that, even as we gain speed and feel most alive, we're actually hurtling toward zero?

10 ♦ Dr. Senegal, I Presume

We cruise a Lawrence, Kansas, neighborhood of picket fences and leafless trees, parking before a small red house, a five-room Sears, Roebuck. Out back on the lawn, short grass and long grass, the manicured shape of a huge penis put there by the owner as a landing pad to welcome the coming space aliens. When we ring the bell, we wait for a moment, for some breathing presence within, then a turn of the knob, and a spectral light frames Harvey's former neighbor in the door, the soon-to-be-late novelist William S. Burroughs.

Father of the Beats, the counterculture incarnate, the junkie poet laureate, Burroughs, along with Allen Ginsberg and Jack Kerouac, were the original rappers about truth and beauty, while opening the door on an underworld world of American drifters, living only for the high of any given moment. Though Harvey once lived around the corner from here, he only ever met Burroughs once, for a lunch arranged by Kevin Hull, the filmmaker. Now, Harvey clasps his hand, enunciating loudly, believing that the eighty-three-year-old Burroughs is hard of hearing, which he isn't, then climbs up the writer's arm until they are in a startled embrace, the two of them as pale as marble.

"REAL, REAL GOOD TO SEE YA!" gushes Harvey.

"Yes, yes, I'm sure I feel likewise, Doctor," says Burroughs. He waves a hand at the clouds, which have just begun to sprinkle ice, squints upward as if expecting pterodactyls, then hurries us inside. Burroughs sits against the wall, in a seat with wheels, the brand name Dynachair emblazoned on it. There is a deep groove in the wall where the back of the chair has rubbed up against it. The writer breathes heavily from his exertion. Prior to our arrival here, Harvey confessed that he tried to read one of Burroughs's books—*Naked Lunch* or *Junky*, he can't remember which—but had no luck. "Couldn't make sense of it," says Harvey. "But they tell me he's some kind of genius."

Burroughs offers Harvey a place at the table next to him, calls in drinks from one of the three men who help keep him tonight, the one named Wayne. Burroughs is dressed in a denim shirt with jeans and a green army coat, which he flicks back to reveal a handgun in a holster over his kidney. He has a bowed back, beautiful blue cat eyes, and cheeks dimpled as if by the tip of a blade. A chaos of wrinkles map his face, an entire life set there: Mexico City. Tangier. Paris. In some groove or deep furrow, too, is the apple he set on his wife's head, like William Tell on peyote, before he accidentally shot her dead. On blue plates before us, cheese, crackers, pepperoni, sardines, and caviar. "Ah yes," he says, "the eggs of sturgeon. A midwestern favorite." Then he loads a mountain of the gooey black baubles on a Saltine. Harvey quaffs glasses of red wine until he turns bright red; Burroughs drains five Coke-and-vodkas after telling us he's just taken his daily dose of methadone.

"WHAT'S THAT?" yells Harvey, having missed Burroughs's pronouncement.

"Methadone, Doctor. An amazing morphine substitution. Have you ever tried morphine?"

"NO. NO, I HAVEN'T," yells Harvey earnestly.

"Unbelievable. In Tangier, there was a most magnificent, most significant drug. . . . Went there just to have the last of it. Last there ever was. Tell me about your addictions, Doctor."

"WAY-ELL, HEH-HEH . . ." But then Harvey says nothing more.

Burroughs lights a joint and offers it to Harvey, who demurs, smoke swirling around his head like a wreath of steam from a Turkish bath.

"DID YOU BECOME ADDICTED BECAUSE YOU FELT PAIN?"

"I wish I could say that, Doctor, but no," says Burroughs. "I became addicted because I wanted more." He considers for a moment, lost behind a white skein. "Now it just gives me something to look forward to."

Harvey nods his head sympathetically but doesn't speak.

"Well, yes, yes, how nice," says Burroughs, addressing the table, thrumming his fingers. He rocks in his Dynachair, takes tiny ballet steps with his toes, fumbles with a Patrick McGrath paperback. He fiddles with his kitty, for the old man loves cats. Above him on a shelf, Laxatone, for feline fur balls; Zantac, for GI upset. The sweet scent of marijuana mingles with the dinner being prepared by someone in the kitchen. Tomato sauce from scratch. Onions and green pepper, steaming off the burgundy. "Well, listen here," says Burroughs, holding up a copy of *Guns & Ammo,* thumbing absently to an ad. "They have a black powder cartridge gun that you can order through the mail. Can you believe this?"

Before Harvey can answer, the writer all of a sudden pops to his feet, starts toward the leather couch and the window above it. Some violent switch has been thrown, though there's nothing here that really suggests danger. Only headlights from the street silently sliding across the walls like flying saucers. "Whazzat?" he growls. Harvey looks startled; Burroughs reaches for his holster. Waves his other hand like he's surrounded by mosquitoes. Avarice, lust, hunger. Wayne rushes in, calms him: Sit down, Master. It's nothing. We have something for you. A little, pretty present.

"A present?" says Burroughs, switching again, dissolving as suddenly into some ecstatic state of childhood. Wayne is in his forties, though wearing an oversized fatigue jacket—the uniform around here—and with his dark sweep of hair, he appears both younger and dwarfish. He leads the writer back to the Dynachair. "Well, well, what could it be?" A happy soft-shoe. Harvey, too, is suddenly piqued, and sits with raised eyebrows—curious cat.

"We'll call it the Bone," says Wayne, disappearing into a dark corner of the house to retrieve it.

"The Bone!" cries Burroughs. "The lovely, lovely Bone!" Harvey is confused now, looking back and forth between Burroughs and Wayne, as Wayne gently places a huge wrapped object on the coffee table. Wayne reads a letter that accompanies it, from an anthropologist who found the following item while trekking in the Southwest. In describing the moment of discovery, the anthropologist writes something like "The object impinged on my periphery." And Burroughs gets stuck on that, starts repeating, "Impinge-on-my-periphery! Impinge-on-my-periphery! Impinge-on-my-periphery!" Then he falls on the gift with greedy hands, disrobing it in a crinkling fury, to reveal—what else?—a large brown petrified bone.

When Harvey sees it, he yells, "IT'S INFILTRATED WITH CALCIUM!" As if it's about to explode, and we all need to take cover. But having worked Harvey up into a climactic frenzy, Burroughs himself has disappeared into a mellow, postcoital reverie. "Absolutely magnificent," he whispers, far away, caressing it. "Feels like linoleum."

Wayne explains. "It's eighty million years old," he says. "The trachodon was a duck-billed dinosaur, a mean fucking dino as big as this house with turds as big as this couch." Burroughs's hands fly up. Delighted. The mere mention of naughty words reminds him of a certain bit of grisliness in Afghanistan, a woman there who was caught having sex with another man not her husband and was stoned to death. "No, they didn't kill her right away," says Burroughs. "Buried to her neck in the ground. Had to drop a heavy rock right on her head like this."

He stands up, throws an invisible rock down with all of his might. Sits. Shudders. Up again. "Like this!" Throws down again. "Terrible." Falls back into the Dynachair, cuddles himself. Up once more. "Like this!" And again. Shiver. Which opens the conversation to killers and gruesome murders. Wayne is a veritable encyclopedia on the topic. He describes a guy in California who raped and mutilated one woman, then killed another, which leads to short bios on Wayne's Hall of Fame of serial killers: Ted Bundy, Charles Ng, and David "Son of Sam" Berkowitz. And there are others, too, set loose and wandering in America right now, huddled by overpasses, buying Twinkies at convenience stores, picking a next victim by the fall of light on her hair as she stands in line at the cash register. When Burroughs seems to be working himself up again, Wayne places some of the writer's own books in front of him to be signed, which works a hypnotic effect. To the anthropologist, he writes: "Thanks for the beautiful bone. Look forward as we look back. All best, William S. Burroughs." It takes a long time to write the note and he repeats it to himself. Again, chanting. "The beautiful bone, the beautiful bone, the beautiful bone."

When he's done he sits back, spent. Harvey, who up until now has been inspecting the trachodon bone, yells, "WHATTA SPECIMEN!" But Burroughs is gone again. The appearance of dinosaurs here, in this gold-colored room, in this Sears, Roebuck house, on this apple-pie block, in this idyllic Kansan town, has set the thin man brooding. So lost in the fireworks of his mind, the body subsists on methadone and caviar. And now as the body fades, it's become an issue of bones. His loss has no end but for the bones.

"Dr. Senegal," says Burroughs, "what good has possibly come from this century?" Harvey swivels in his seat, assuming that another physician has arrived, then realizes that Burroughs is now addressing him as Dr. Senegal. He makes a show of deep consideration.

"WAY-ELL, THERE HAVE BEEN REAL IMPROVEMENTS IN MENTAL HEALTH."

"Chemical improvements?"

"NOT JUST CHEMICAL—"

But then Burroughs interrupts. "No, Doctor, nothing good will come from the End. More of a police state. More crime. More attacks on queers. I hope not to be here for it."

And he won't be. In a few months he'll be dead. But now, he's bewildered, jigging to some distant music in his mind. Since we haven't planned to stay for dinner, we get ready to leave, though once he's gotten started on the End, Burroughs has much to say. Computer chips lodged in the brains of newborn infants, poets lynched in the trees along magnolia-lined driveways to Corporate Headquarters, a howling pandemonium of neo-Nazis, hip-hop brothers, born-agains, and Black Muslims all getting to know one another in the city streets of America with automatic weapons. It appears Harvey has never considered the matter from this angle, and seems a bit stunned. But then Wayne intervenes.

"Ah, William," he says fondly, "it won't be that bad." He helps Burroughs from the Dynachair and then Burroughs leads us to the front door. On the tippy front porch, finally, Harvey and Burroughs face each other for a good-bye. The writer lowers his voice and delivers a farewell chestnut, one that Harvey receives with a knowing nod, though it isn't clear he actually hears it.

"What keeps the old alive, Dr. Senegal," whispers Burroughs, "is that we learn to be evil."

And then we are out in the night, in a downpour, Harvey trundling toward the car for what feels like a small eternity. Behind him, Burroughs sways, curling and unfurling his arms like elephant trunks, then assumes a position of Buddhist prayer—pale, delirious, still.

⚛

If I believed that coming to Lawrence would be a kind of homecoming for Harvey—he spent six years living in this area and left only a year ago to move in with Cleora—then it's a strange one. Yes, the gods have heaped almost biblical weather on us. After visiting Burroughs, we go downtown for dinner, and Harvey literally falls up to his knee in ice water when he inadvertently steps in a rushing gutter to cross the street. "WHOA, WHOA, YOW!" he yells, then hops around in a circle, pant leg soaked, flashes of lightning exploding over his head. But, after that excitement, there are so few other dramas on the nostalgia tour. He has decided he doesn't want to visit the plastics factory where he worked just a year ago, a job he took to make ends meet after his medical license was revoked, but he tells me that both his job and his coworkers there were "real, real interesting."

Later, when I get in touch with Harvey's old boss, a supervisor named William Katz at a place called E & E Display Group, I learn more about Harvey's tenure in the plastics trade. Katz enthusiastically traces Harvey's meteoric rise through the factory—from assembler to extruder's apprentice to extruder operator, the person who works the downstream end of an extruder, a machine that produces the angled plastic shelving most often used to hold Hallmark cards. As an extruder operator, he made eight dollars an hour. Even after getting hit by the old woman in her car and breaking his leg, Harvey still returned to the full vigors of the job, clambering up ten-foot ladders to check the hopper without a whinny of complaint.

"I had no idea Tom was a physician," says Katz, "but I recognized he was a man of integrity. Literate and witty. And tough. I don't care whether he was cutting up brains or making plastic parts, I loved the guy." Katz discovered his extruder operator's secret in a Kansas University student newspaper that ran a story on the parade of pilgrims that were coming to Lawrence to see Harvey and Einstein's brain. "I brought the article in, showed Tom, and said, 'This must be a hoax.' He was kind of embarrassed, but he said, 'Well, yeah, it's true.' He told me about being a pathologist in New Jersey when Einstein died. He said he took it as his personal mission to see if there was some physical evidence of Einstein's genius, but that he hadn't found anything definitive. Said he kept the brain in the closet."

While Harvey's critics claim that the pathologist was showboating with Einstein's brain, supposedly counting coup, it somehow doesn't compute. In fact, on closer inspection, it's amazing how few people, even those who considered themselves friends of Harvey, knew that he had Einstein's brain in the first place, and amazing, too, how expertly Harvey obscured whole lagoons and volcanoes and mountains of himself in rain forest, how he lived life as a hologram. It's a fact reaffirmed by our visit earlier in the day to a Lawrence food co-op where he once volunteered on a regular basis. The cars in the parking lot there are festooned with bumper stickers: Free Tibet. Free Leonard Peltier. Free Experimental Lab Rats. Free Love. "Real nice place," says Harvey when we push through the door. "Good sandwiches, I recall." Then he gets lost in the herb section, among bottles of echinacea and kava kava.

It's the standard funky, crunchy co-op, the kind most often found in university towns, brightly lit, with refrigerated units overflowing with arugula and carrots. There's nary a soul working here over thirty: a ragged nation of unshaven faces and odoriferous armpits, tattoos and pierced eyebrows. Ani Difranco on the stereo, everything smelling of cumin and brown rice. A few of the workers fake-smile when they see Harvey, regard him as another customer, albeit one from planet Old Guy, and a few more register a look of vague recognition. Eventually a woman wearing beads and an earth-mother skirt approaches, scratches her head at the sight of Harvey, and says, "Hey, yeah—what happened to you, anyway?" In the barrage of modern life, no one here seems to remember the old man's name.

"Heh-heh . . . I moved," says Harvey.

"Oh," says the woman. "Well, it's good to see you." And she glides gracefully toward the cash registers. "You, too," says Harvey, almost as an afterthought. He expects no more, or less. He slouches before a wall of elixirs, takes down a bottle of Happy Wanderer, and reads the label. He meanders the aisles, taking stock of the shelves he used to stock, performing scientific analysis. "This used to be over there," he says, holding up a box of couscous.

Watching him, I can't help but think of my favorite Ingmar Bergman film, *Wild Strawberries,* in which an old doctor, Isak, drives through Sweden with his young daughter-in-law on his way to a ceremony in his honor. Near the end of his life, Isak is a cantankerous old cuss, but along the road, he revisits his past—the summer cottage of his youth, the people and places of his life—and some stubborn glacier in him begins to melt. He releases his ghosts like so many birds and awkwardly tries to reembrace the days he has left to him. But the thing is this: Despite his road-trip epiphanies, Isak isn't suddenly free or whole or pure or completely absolved. He is inescapably himself, full of both love and hate, scarred by betrayal and yet still fueled by longing, hurtling toward his own death.

Harvey seems to travel through life with far fewer regrets. If he's a sinner, he doesn't seem to know it yet. If he's a car, then he's the one doing fifty-five in the right-hand lane of the highway, forgetfully, unapologetically, flashing a blinker he long ago acted on—and he's been on this highway for over forty years. If he's a house, then he's one with lots of disconnected additions, each new one built in six- and seven-year spurts—full of new wives, kids, and jobs, the only constant being the wallpaper, pink floral blooms of brain floating to the ceiling.

After a pasta dinner, we go to visit one of Dr. Harvey's very best friends, Ahilleas Maurellis—Archie. A thirty-five-year-old bulk of body with a haywire ponytail and the fleshy pressed-together features of his Greek ancestry, he's Harvey's old roommate from the last two years of Harvey's Lawrence idyll. They met at a Quaker friends' meeting. I'm told that Archie is a brilliant physics graduate student, that he speaks five or six languages and is an accomplished musician. Though his five-room apartment—what was once Harvey's apartment, too—is of grad-school pedigree (everything generic or slightly shabby except for the hi-fi system), he is a man of fine tastes. An aficionado of wines and music, beauty and art. He puffs his cigarettes with sophistication, blowing smoke in the shape of hippopotami.

Some years ago, on a losing streak with women, he found a computer Web site that helped arrange long-distance relationships with women in the Ukraine. He made one trip there, hit pay dirt with a special lady, got engaged, but when that dalliance suddenly hit the skids, he returned and claimed another, the blond woman standing next to him now. The two have fallen together like songbirds and will marry in the summer.

Harvey returns to them as a conquering hero, warmly embraced by Archie at the door. Behind the two hugging men stand Archie's mother and grandmother, who just happen to be visiting from Greece. Archie's grandmother is about Harvey's age, though at first she looks much older. She wears a sequined black bathrobe and keeps her hair in a net. She is also hard of hearing, but this time it's her grandson who turns up the volume. "THIS IS TOM HARVEY, GRANDMA. YOU KNOW, MY FRIEND WHO HAS EINSTEIN'S BRAIN." At that, her eyes flash white, as if a thousand snow geese of recognition have suddenly taken flight from some hidden lake in her pupil. She only has a few teeth left and speaks with a heavy accent. "Thith man," she says, "wasth de last to touch de great Profthessor Einth-stein. He isth . . . famous."

Harvey blushes, pleased. "It's real, real good to see you," he says, and goes to shake her hand. "Wonderful," he says. But Archie's grandmother brushes right by his outstretched hand, plants a kiss on his cheek. When he moves toward the living room, she shadows him like a schoolgirl. When he goes to sit on the couch she nearly trips him up, falls next to him on the cushions, sandwiching him between her own self and Archie's mother. As far as I can tell, Harvey isn't wearing animal aftershave. But clearly he glows with something luminous, for the woman is certifiably and spontaneously starry for him. He accepts a brandy from Archie, who sits down and says, "So, tell us what's new with life, love, and brain?"

"Way-ell," drawls Harvey. "I'm in New Jersey now." When Archie asks where he lives exactly, he alludes to "a friend who was kind

enough to offer living quarters," but doesn't offer any more information about Cleora. When Archie asks him about the nature of my in-
volvement on this road trip, Harvey briskly says, "He's my chauffeur."
And when Archie asks about Einstein's brain, Harvey tells him the
brain is fine and that "the study" is proceeding. As he speaks, Archie's
grandmother absently runs her forefinger up and down Harvey's leg,
tracing his femur. Then, she turns to Archie and asks if the rest of us
might leave her alone with the doctor.

"UHHH . . . NO, GRANDMA," says Archie, smiling. "WE'RE ALL
HAVING A LITTLE GET-TOGETHER. WE'RE ALL TALKING TO
TOM." He speaks with a perfect, well-mannered British accent, and at
the same time can't keep his hands off his own blond minx, as she
can't keep hers from him. Which seems to incite matters back on the
couch. The only people left on the sidelines are me and Archie's
mother, a short sixtyish woman with a mole on her chin. We catch
each other's eye, but it's not going to happen. Archie apologizes to
Harvey for his grandmother.

Then he lights a cigarette, puts on a CD of Ukrainian folk music,
and goes to get some ice at the same time that I head to the kitchen
for a refill of wine. Away from Harvey, Archie and I have a chat about
the brain. He tells me that when the two men were roommates,
Harvey occasionally kept the brain out on the kitchen table, but only
when he was working on it. "It was weird having it here at first. I
mean it was hard to eat lunch with it around," confides Archie in a
loud voice. It seems there are no secrets between Harvey and him.
"Like you're eating a ham sandwich and you're staring at this big
piece of ham, but it just happens to be, you know, *Einstein's brain.*"
He says there were many people that came to the apartment from
around the world—camera crews, journalists, and pilgrims, South
Africans, Brazilians, and Japanese. "He's something of a famous
man," says Archie, dramatically shooting cigarette smoke from the
side of his mouth, motioning through the wall to Harvey. "And he's
a fine, fine person. Just one of the best."

It's a refrain I'll hear again and again. When I speak to Patrick McAlinney, Harvey's former partner in a general practice the two once shared in the Kansas City area, he describes Harvey as "a cautious, conservative physician who was nothing but a gentleman." And from the Princeton days, fellow doctor Lewis Fishman says, "He is a scholarly man, the cream of physicians, honest and sincere. His personal life has been tragic. Now he's practically broke. He's spent all his money educating his children from various marriages. He's a heck of a nice guy."

When we return to the living room, Archie's grandmother is hanging on Harvey's every word—though she hears none of them. She sits pucker-mouthed and sequined, hand on the great doctor's knee, amorously batting her eyes at him, then staring distractedly into the center of the room, slightly cross-eyed. "Oh, Tom . . . oh, Tom," she murmurs every so often. Meanwhile, Harvey is engaged with Archie's fiancée, trying to get to know her. "I sure like that Ukrainian music," he says meaningfully. Archie's fiancée seems transfixed, too. And when Archie sees the domestic scene before him, he smiles at me, as if all is right with the world. But then, just after we sit, after we begin to let ourselves unwind, after Harvey's polished off his glass of brandy, he's suddenly antsy. Just like that. Forty-five minutes and he's ready to ramble.

Still, he's wedged so tightly between Archie's folks that the process takes a while, and once Grandma sees the big *Doctor Zhivago* goodbye coming, she tightens her grip. What amazes me is that maybe half her passion is meant for someone else—Einstein—while Harvey is just the courtly proxy. And it's amazing, too, that there are people like her walking this earth today, still enthralled by a man long dead. After Einstein's second wife, Elsa, died, he received a number of marriage proposals. "How much brighter my existence would be," wrote one woman, "if I could persuade you that we both should be happier were we to unite in cheering each other's daily path." And another, a friend of Elsa's from Vienna begins: "A secret voice in my innermost soul (which rarely deceives me) tells me that I must devote my life to you. . . . It is my deepest wish to give Professor Einstein the most beautiful evening of life."

The best the women can do is extract a promise from Harvey that he'll come visit them in Greece someday soon. There will be swimming and olives for everyone! Harvey promises, Archie's grandmother still clamped to his arm. To the end, he's obligingly chivalrous. A celebrity once-removed, driving his groupies agog, but then not flaunting it, and not asking for it, either.

There is an awkward moment when everything that this evening had once promised is extinguished for Archie's grandmother. The unspoken words spill out like fish on a dry pier, shimmering, flailing, dying there. For it's late. The clock is tired. And Harvey is moving toward the door. Even with dead weight on his arm, he is beginning to float above and beyond. This renegade pathologist newly christened Senegal, this unfettered maker of plastic shelving for Hallmark cards. Grandma sparkles once. *I love the way you love . . . Mr. Wonderful Person . . . us forever.* Then her grandson pries her from Harvey. She holds her smile as we descend the stairs, curling downward toward Earth. She holds it until the last split second when Harvey moves out of her eye, and she out of his, until she realizes he's gone.

11 ◆ Whazzat?

We stay at a place called the Westminster Hotel, out on the edge of Lawrence, near the flyover to Interstate 70. But for the British flair of the name, it's your typical two-story, no-frills, prefab roadside affair. The walls are thin and papered with cowboys. As usual, we take adjoining rooms, and once I'm sure Harvey is settled, I go back to my own room and try to call Sara. Though I let the phone ring, it's futile. She's not home—again and again.

But then where is she?

It's a simple question but once it's been asked, a floodgate of questions follow: What if something's happened? Back in Maine, we live miles from a town, miles from a hospital, miles from good people who might come to her rescue if anything went awry. Or what if she's run off the road? Before I left, she'd hit a patch of black ice going fifty in the pickup we share and done a 180. And moose. Moose are as plentiful as squirrels in Maine. Big, lurking, thousand-pound behemoths just waiting to pounce on a passing vehicle. Who would know if she'd hit one in a snowstorm and needed help?

Once I exhaust the doomsday stuff, I find more: What if she's *gone* gone? Like, packed up and left? Just got fed up (who could blame her?) and called it quits (finally) and when the phone rings now (her sad boyfriend in a sad hotel room with an old man and a chopped-up brain through the wall), it rings next to a note, written in her hand on some random letterhead collected during her various stays at random foreign hotels, saying sayonara, good luck. A letter in a room of inanimate objects never to be animated again by Us Together. And this thought leads me mercilessly into a mourning so deep I find myself grieving an end that is all but hypothetical and yet so real I can touch its face.

Days pass and months pass and years pass and you light the holy candle of yourself by the glimmer of someone else, and just when you think you're burned out on her, you realize that she's the single thing that raises you above yourself. And now she's dumped you flat and taken up with a lumberjack or that sensitive guy in town who runs the bookstore or the FedEx man who wears tight shorts in the summer. That guy? How could she?

And what about our dog, Trout? The thought of them, the three of them together hiking the White Mountains, drinking from one water container, speaking their own nonsensical, dovey language, is too much. And the way people just pick up and immediately reconstruct a life with someone else, as if their life with you never mattered—how dare she?

What I do then is what I do best when my mind begins such stark spiraling: I distract myself. I try to think of people to call, dial two or three phone numbers but get only answering machines. I decide to touch base with Evelyn Einstein out in Berkeley, California.

"Hello?" She answers the phone as a half question and a half challenge, the way I suppose any Einstein might who's had their share of cranks and bizarros call late at night, obsessed with Albert, spewing nonsense. We've spoken twice before now—once when I was in Maine, and once when I was in Princeton—and Evelyn's tentatively agreed to meet Dr. Harvey, though, from the start she's seemed less than enthusiastic about the prospect. When I tell her that Harvey and I have made it to Kansas, she lets out a deep sigh, as if toppled by a wave of inevitability. "I don't know," she says, "my house is a mess."

"Don't worry about cleaning it," I say, staring up to the corner of the room, to where the wallpaper is peeling and several upside-down cowboys seem to defy gravity. "You're not dealing with neat freaks here. Or if you'd rather not . . ." I offer to try to find someone to come clean for her, or, I suggest, we could meet on neutral ground, in a restaurant somewhere, but it turns out that the issue is less the cleaning than her health.

Evelyn tells me that she's sick and has a hard time moving around. Some years ago, she was treated for cancer with steroids and now she believes they're ravaging her body, eating her own healthy cells, destroying her liver. "You could run a herd of elephants on the steroids they gave me," she says. "HMOs are vile."

We talk for a while, the conversation listing from alien invasions to cults. "I'm sure there are plenty of cults that would love to get their hands on Albie's brain," says Evelyn. "When I was a cult deprogrammer, I was amazed at how they fed on the suggestible by quoting my grandfather." A cult deprogrammer? The question opens a can of interesting worms, for Evelyn admits she was damn good at her job. What she learned after years in the business is that cults are everywhere, waiting for you, because, whether or not you know it just yet, you're missing something, searching for something, or someone, for Mommy or Daddy, for God or the devil, to deliver you. She admits that she was one of those people, too, shunted by her father, Hans Albert, who only had a mind for his hydrology and sailing, brushing his daughter aside as he himself had been brushed aside by his father, Albert. And so Evelyn was simply lost for many years.

"I went through EST," she says, "and I was terrified. They were trying to get me because it was good advertising to have an Einstein. People think you have to be feebleminded, but that's malarkey. It's so deceptively easy to get people to stop trusting their own senses. They cut you off and then put fear in you. They say, remember so-and-so who left six months ago, she got hit by a car. One day a light went on, and I thought, 'Jesus, this is how Hitler did it.' "

That's when she escaped and started working for the other side. She says she was followed everywhere by crazy cultists. She had her house staked out by cultists. And when she freed a good friend from one cult, she found herself being chased through a New York hotel by more cultists. "If I had my health," she says to me now, "I'd still be working to stop them."

Evelyn is just getting started, it seems, when I'm suddenly gripped by paranoia. I gingerly extricate myself from the conversation, and when I hang up the phone, I sit for a moment thinking. I can't shake the image of two bullying headlights that were blazing in our rearview on the drive to Burroughs's, and then again on the way back from Archie's. Is it my paranoia or has it been the same set of lights since Princeton?

I go to the window and peer through the thick drapes. In the parking lot below, there's a car with its engine chuffing, headlights extinguished, and exhaust pouring from its back end. The mere apparition of that car sets my mind racing. I imagine a man peering up from behind a fogged windshield at our two rooms, smoking butts, coldly eating doughnuts, muttering in some foreign tongue on a cell phone, biding time.

I find myself pacing. I turn on the TV, volume low, and sit at the end of the bed, stock-straight, spider senses tingling. Everything is absolutely still in the room except for the ball at the end of the lamp chain, swinging. Then swinging back. It really could be anyone out there. I go to the wall and listen for Harvey, but hear nothing. And I catch myself in the mirror over the sink looking pale with dark rings under my eyes, connected again to every other slightly nauseated soul in a motel room looking panic-stricken in a mirror.

A televangelist named Bob Larson appears on a local access station, waving an issue of *Rolling Stone* with Goth-rock icon Marilyn Manson on the cover. For some reason, this calms me. "Our fifth graders are being seduced by Satan," he bellows. He has gun-barrel eyes, a fast-moving mouth, and flashes of sharp teeth. "We're going to beat the devil . . . but there is NO TIME!" Manson stares out from *Rolling Stone* with one ice-blue eye, one black, each popped as if he's a lizard being squeezed round the waist, his black lips parted slightly, gazing from a dark, abstract pool of makeup that trails to sharp points. He might have just crawled from the muck of Atchafalaya. The Dark Prince who, it was rumored, had some of his ribs removed so he could give himself a blow job. The Mephistopheles who was arrested for having another man's penis in his mouth onstage. The sinister, deviant, fellating merchant of End-of-the-world-ism.

By contrast, Bob Larson is fifty-ish with a strange, anvil-shaped wedge of hair and a G.I. Joe beard. Rolled-up sleeves and a loosened tie. Furry knuckles. Bat-wing eyebrows. The carefully coiffed dishevelment of a man so completely given over to his Maker, you must entrust him with some percentage of your earnings. He is broadcasting from a room that looks like a radio studio, and the metal blinds are half open, revealing cars passing on some suburban Denver street. He is oddly comforting, like a military father who saves his progeny from ever having to make a decision of their own.

A teenager named Rusty calls. His friend has been possessed by Satan, and Rusty has bought Bob's book on Satan, called *In the Name of Satan*, and is performing an exorcism at this very moment, but the demon is not leaving his friend. Bob Larson's face scrunches into an expression of great concern. "Use the book, Rusty," he hisses. "And the other book." Waves the Bible, almost as an afterthought.

A call from Peoria. A call from Des Moines. The devil's everywhere. Responding to Pete from Tallahassee, who has just been successfully exorcised of Satan, Bob Larson sets out his agenda for America, one predicated on the destruction of all heavy-metal music and the obliteration of Marilyn Manson. As well as booming sales of his book, *In the Name of Satan*.

"Are you with me?" asks Bob Larson. "Do you believe in the power of the Word?" He holds up his book again. Forgets the Bible this time.

It's like this, watched over by Bob Larson, protected by the Word, that I drift out to sea on a riptide of dream. In one, Harvey and I are lost in the medina of an ancient city, scrambling through labyrinthian streets with a sack slung over my shoulder, chased by men in black hoods. In another, the sack appears again but this time there is no Harvey, just an old man, a beggar, it seems, who warns me not to look inside the sack. I seem to be on a long journey somewhere, and for as long as I can, I heed his caution. But then my patience runs out and I untie the sack, and when I finally look inside I'm devoured by light.

Much later, I wake with a start, with my feet planted on the floor, still wearing my clothes. The first gray illumination of day filters through the curtains; the television is a field of wiggly static. And there's knocking at the door. How long has it been going on?

I rise groggily, with that foreboding feeling you get when suddenly shocked from sleep. In my mind, I rummage through several quick scenarios, including the one in which my compadre left hours ago with a man in a black cape and cowl. But then, when I throw open the door, it's . . . Harvey!

"I packed my bag," he says, "but you didn't come get me."

I gaze at the old man, wrapped in a scarf, his eyes pink around the rim. Harvey, the Energizer Bunny, against bales of blowing snow.

I want to hug him, but instead we agree to go for breakfast.

⚛

The snow is nuclear-powered, driving horizontally, starring the windows with ice, piling up until the Skylark looks like a soap-flake duck float in a Memorial Day parade gone terribly wrong. Everything is heaped in the frigid no-smell of winter, cars skidding, then running off roadsides into gullies. The snow falls in thick sheaves, icicles jag tree branches, like the memory of a day 500,000 years ago when all of Kansas was freeze-dried under hundreds of feet of ice.

It's packed at the Village Inn Pancake House: college students and the elderly and everyone in between: all flannel-shirted how-are-ya's ricocheting everywhere, steak-and-egg specials zooming by on superwhite plates. Some of the old men wear work pants and base-ball caps with automotive labels; the undergrads sport caps embla-zoned with team names or slogans like Whatever or Good to Go or Rage. Even in the No Smoking section everyone smokes—one of Harvey's pet peeves. And yet, there's so much warmth in numbers this morning, so much well-being, that it's hard to hold a grudge. Outside, it's howling, and inside we're basking in the golden light of camaraderie and flapjacks.

Take your hallowed halls of Congress or the littered floor of the Stock Exchange, America is built on its pancake houses!

Our restaurant routine usually follows a familiar pattern, which doesn't waver this morning: Harvey meditates over the menu, exam-ining it, dissecting, vectoring, and equating what his stomach really wants. Meanwhile, I get a newspaper and skim a few sections before he's ready to order. Even as two teenagers have been indicted for the murder and dismemberment of a man in Central Park, there's an on-going existential debate raging in Harvey's head: salty or sweet, eggs or waffles.

Occasionally, after a particularly deliberate order, he'll deliberately change it. Luckily, our waitress is a pathologically smiley KU student, well-versed in the dynamics of a breakfast rush, the coffee-craving, caffeine-induced chaology of it all. She waits as Harvey takes a sec-ond look at the menu. It could be that an actual week passes as he clears his throat a couple of times, then ponders some more, but she smiles patiently and then chirps back, "Eggs over easy, bacon, wheat toast, home fries. More coffee?"

It's hard to imagine that fine people like her were blown to smithereens twenty years ago in a nuclear attack concocted for a panic-inspiring, made-for-television movie starring Jason Robards, called *The Day After*. The few who survived wandered in a post-apocalyptic stupor, in rags, bodies flowered with keloid scars, trying to find a shot glass of clean water. That Lawrence would become connected in the nation's psyche with nuclear devastation, and that Einstein's brain, the power that unknowingly wrought the bomb, resided here for many years under Harvey's midwestern protectorship, is a small pixel of irony that seems to escape Harvey. When I ask him about it, he says, "Way-ell, I guess that's true, all right."

The truth is that Einstein himself was confounded by the idea that his theory of relativity had opened up a Pandora's box of assured annihilation. In a 1935 press conference, in which he was asked about the possibility of building an atomic bomb, Einstein said that the likelihood of transforming matter into energy was "something akin to shooting birds in the dark in a country where there are only a few birds." In retrospect, the comment shows just how far out of step Einstein was with the science of his day, how lost he was in his own stubborn, theoretical isolationism. But then, in the world's eyes, Einstein had become much more than a scientist. If the time of his greatest discoveries ran between the years 1905 and 1925, then the last thirty years of his life, while no less dedicated to research, gave rise to Einstein the political creature, an outspoken, though avuncular presence who, for many, possessed as much moral authority as genius.

Four years later, however, as the Nazi war machine began to move on Europe, Leo Szilard and Enrico Fermi presented Einstein with a clear explanation for how a bomb could be built. In a letter dated August 2, 1939, Einstein, the celebrated pacifist, urged President Roosevelt to go forward immediately with the building of an atomic weapon. "In the course of the last four months," writes Einstein to the President, "it has been made probable . . . that it may become possible to set up a nuclear chain reaction [sic] in a large mass of uranium, by which vast amounts of power and large quantities of new radium-like elements would be generated. Now it appears almost certain that this could be achieved in the immediate future."

Einstein goes on to outline delivery systems for the bomb: "A single bomb of this type, carried by boat and exploded in a port, might very well destroy the whole port together with some of the surrounding territory. However, such bombs might very well prove to be too heavy for transportation by air." And then he worries over the world's uranium supplies: "The United States has only very poor area of uranium [sic] in moderate quantities. There is some good ore in Canada and the former Czechoslovakia, while the most important source of uranium is Belgian Congo."

When the letter was delivered to Roosevelt, the President at first responded slowly but soon realized the gravity of the situation—if the Americans had just thought to build a bomb, perhaps the Nazis, with great scientists such as Heisenberg, were well on their way to completing one—and commanded his chief of staff to begin top-secret plans for the building of an atomic weapon. In 1942, on an empty mesa in New Mexico, rose the Town That Never Was—Los Alamos—and, under the guidance of scientist Robert Oppenheimer, came Little Boy and Fat Man, the bombs that would eventually decimate Hiroshima and Nagasaki, respectively.

Because Einstein aroused such great suspicion—even within the Roosevelt White House, where his outspokenness deemed him untrustworthy—he was not asked to join Oppenheimer's team. In fact, he had nothing to do with the bomb whatsoever, though Oppenheimer and others later used his letter to consecrate their efforts, as if Einstein himself had endorsed not just the building of the bomb but the dropping of bombs on both Hiroshima and Nagasaki. In fact, that one letter to Roosevelt haunted Einstein until the end of his life and endangered at least one family member, Hans Albert, who was once physically attacked during a speech by a man who blamed his father for the bomb. Later, Einstein told Linus Pauling that the letter was the "one mistake" of his life. When the bomb was dropped on Hiroshima—on August 6, 1945—he heard the news on vacation, after waking from a nap at Saranac Lake. "Oy vay," he said wearily. "Alas."

❊

After breakfast, we brave the elements. Buffeted by high winds in the parking lot, Harvey's hair swirling in a little tornado on his head, we reclaim the Skylark from the encroaching glacier and wing back on Interstate 70 heading west. Worried for our cargo, I ask if maybe we should let the brain ride in the passenger compartment rather than the trunk for fear that it will freeze solid. But Harvey doesn't respond, remains completely silent, neither miffed nor pleased, zenning out in the blizzard. Then twenty miles down the road, the snow suddenly slows to mere ticks, and a white light begins to fill space in the sky, prying open the clouds. As it will happen in this single day, we will live through four seasons. Which can occur if one drives long enough with Einstein's brain in the trunk. Time bends, accelerates, and overlaps; it moves backward, vertically, then loops; simultaneity rules.

My strategy has been to keep the Skylark at seventy-five or eighty, scanning the road for cops, and when feeling luxurious or bored rotten to push it to eighty-five max. Which is precisely what I get nailed for—eighty-five in a sixty-five-mile-per-hour zone. Sirens blare and Harvey looks a bit ill. The trooper in his cruiser herds us up an exit ramp—for what reason I don't know—and then comes sidling up the driver's side. I watch him in the side-view, striding purposefully in unscuffed black Mountie boots. I roll down my window and stick my head out of the car.

"How are you today, sir?" I say.

"Place your head back in the car," he says tersely. He asks for my documents—license and registration—which I produce. He takes both, eyes them suspiciously, then asks me to join him in his car. He escorts me back to his Crown Vic cruiser where George Jones blares on the radio. I don't defend my actions, the greed of speed. "Where you boys going in such a hurry?" he asks. Glancing into the Skylark's back window, I can just make out the silver crown of Harvey's head. I'm overcome with the desire to confess. It's not exactly as if we have a dead body stashed in the trunk, but then it's not as if we don't, either.

"California," I say.

"What for?"

"Um, family . . . reunion . . . vacation."

The trooper raises an eyebrow.

"Family reunion," I say.

But then the trooper doesn't really seem to care. He's done the arithmetic, and with Harvey in the front seat, helpless in the red strobe light, we don't look like drug runners any more than we look like two hombres packing Einstein's brain. He writes out the ticket, warns me against trying eighty-five again in his state, and sets me free. When he turns off the road in the opposite direction, taking George Jones with him, we're sitting on top of an overpass, looking out on the awesome beauty of the naked plains that stretch to the pressed-down edge of the horizon. There's nothing in sight to our left, and nothing to our right but a road heading north.

So we take it.

Part Three

12 ◆ The Garden of Eden

The road is gold and mystical, running smack-dab along the geolog-
ical middle of America, the seam where the West untethers from the
East so that nothing, nothing will look like the East again. We're at
the place where the light begins to hit the cross-country freight trains
differently, in longer, brilliant rays, in candescent orange, and then
the shadows lay purple over everything, fall in wondrous, warm-rain
plagues over the small-town bankers and waitresses leaving their
cafés, bundled in polar fleece. Everyone seems equal in this light and
shadow, this rich, penniless air.

We're at the place, too, where the sky gets large and wild with big
whusping castles of clouds, where things become more of an im-
provisation: trailer homes haphazardly laid out on wide plateaus surrounded by payloads and jubilees of junk—old, rusted gas
refrigerators from Dust Bowl times, bedsprings on which generations have been conceived and born, eaten-through cars, the ravaged
sites of so many first dates and first kisses and funeral processions.
All these ghosts come alive as we pass some invisible Maginot Line,
as the American mind moves from the imprisoning whimsy of cities
through some harder-boiled practicality to the eagle flight of the
West.

The snow has left us now. The earth is an umber color. And there's
still a hard wind that seems to gain speed over the endless miles of
nothingness, wrapping some occasional piece of loose ruffage—

sagebrush or cheatgrass—and then absently spinning it like a wagon wheel. Until we cut ourselves loose of the rushing interstate, I hadn't realized what a relief it would be for our little cult of three to get lost on a tributary. And so here we are.

All of this emptiness prompts Harvey to wax about his second wife, Alison. After they split, he was astounded by what she became, by her life after Harvey. "She started up with investing, you know," says Harvey. "Real smart girl, financial mind. Had her own company down there in Florida, I think. Made lots of money. Died of cancer." I ask a few questions, to draw him out, and he doesn't resist. She was from Australia, a stewardess. They met in Kansas years after she'd quit flying. Harvey courted her and they married—then who really knows what happened? But that familiar growing distance came like two parting canyon walls whittled by wind. Whether or not Einstein's brain had something to do with it, they split. That's it. And well, heh-heh, she made lots of money afterward. "That girl," says Harvey, "a real sharp mind, it turns out."

After some miles we come to a stop sign in the middle of nowhere and turn left. Not far up the road is the tiny town of Lucas, Kansas, with its five hundred peace-loving citizens and the fabled Brant's Meat Market, where according to a tourist brochure celebrating the highlights of Lucas one can "sample some of Doug's homemade bologna fresh from the smokehouse." But what's caught our eye are the signs pointing to a place called the Garden of Eden. Built at the beginning of the century, the garden is the brainchild of "an American maverick," Samuel Perry Dinsmoor. In our national parlance, what's usually meant by the word "maverick" is someone who skirts the edge of sanity—or is so insane as to appear sane—who then does something absolutely insane and yet, after the passage of time, and especially if the maverick's creation yields a profit of any kind, is deemed less and less insane until the maverick worms his or her way into the fibers of history. Then generations grow to envy the ingenuity and courage of the maverick while glossing over the maverick's genetic kookiness. On such shoulders, a country rises.

S. P. Dinsmoor does not disappoint. As a grizzled old codger, he fashioned over one hundred tons of cement into a "log cabin" and then kept right on going, building his own version of the Garden of Eden, complete with about thirty cement trees and fifty sculptures. The garden itself looks a little like a jungle gym, the rough-hewn expression of something from the mind of a third grader. We join on to a tour led by a very friendly woman named Darla who looks vaguely like Bob Dole, who himself grew up not that far from here, in Russell. She says "cee-mint" for "cement," a word that repeats itself fetishistically around the Garden of Eden. Along with Harvey and me are two retired men who've rolled in from downstate. The one wearing a yellow windbreaker has already been to the Garden a few times in the last couple years, but just itching to get back, he's decided to brave the weather today and make the pilgrimage with his buddy, a first-timer wearing brand-new bright-white Reebok walking shoes.

Our guide takes to heart her serious role as teacher, historian, and folk entertainer, and lays Dinsmoor's story on thick as cheese curd, old-fashioned and a little lumpy. A Civil War vet who claimed to have witnessed General Lee's surrender, a farmer, and a populist politician, Dinsmoor settled in Lucas and died here in 1932. "Seems ole Mr. Dinsmoor had a few thoughts about things," says Darla. And here she pauses a moment, raises an ironic eyebrow, gestures to the cement jungle about us, coaching us along to the fact that Dinsmoor, the old fire-breather, had a whole footlocker full of nutty opinions. "He wasn't a fan of the eagle as national bird. But let me direct your eyes above." The retirees appear startled, look up. "Feast your eyes on the cement American flag, and you'll find a cement turkey as counterbalance. What's that I said? That's right: turkey! Ole Dinsmoor believed the turkey should be our national bird!"

The retirees look dumbstruck. The first-timer pulls out a case and switches the glasses he wears for new ones, then takes a second gander. He shakes his head. "Did the local folk not consider this man bizarre?" he asks.

The tour guide smiles and then affects a chuckle. "Oh, ha, ha, ha . . . Yea-sss, they sure did. Ole Mr. Dinsmoor was famous for his, shall we say, aberrations in behavior." Again the eyebrow, an ironic purse of the lips, then she's off and running on more canned facts. She tells us how Dinsmoor tapped the town's water main to make a small wading pool, how he went on wild drinking binges and took to cavorting with young girls in town, evidenced by a number of cement young girls in the garden, and finally how he married his first wife on horseback, then after the old lady passed on, how he took his twenty-year-old Czechoslovakian housekeeper as his second wife, and at the spry age of eighty-one got down to the steamy business of making a couple more kids.

Again, the retirees stand mouths agape; the one in the yellow windbreaker has apparently forgotten most of Dinsmoor's biography from his previous visits, or is just swept up in the drama of it now, because he's clearly as scandalized as his buddy. True, old Dinsmoor was no looker—hoary-bearded, wall-eyed, head like a bashed-in jack-o'-lantern—and he was no Michelangelo, either. But for these men, it seems to be a moral thing. When I steal a glance at Harvey, standing a little apart from the crowd, he's smiling, but only when I notice his shoulders barely moving up and down do I realize he's actually giggling. Very lightly, but yes—giggling.

Darla continues. She points out angels and devils, a big eye, which is meant to be the eye of God, and storks equipped with lightbulbs in their mouths and baby faces under their wings. There's a reason for everything here, much of it described from Dinsmoor's own book about the Garden, entitled *The Cabin Home*. About his concrete Cain and Abel, Dinsmoor claims Cain was raising pumpkins but "the Lord didn't like rotten pumpkins. I don't blame Him." Abel, on the other hand, offered God "a dandy little buck-merino" and the Lord liked "good mutton." So that's when Cain got the idea to knock off Abel. "He couldn't have killed him with a gun," reasons Dinsmoor. "I just imagine he got Abel out in the 'tater patch and brained him with his hoe."

When Darla shows us Adam and Eve, who stand ten feet tall as a gate entrance to the bower, she flashes a sly look. "You can tell that some of the cement is newer on Adam and Eve than the other cement," she says, a bald reference to two loincloths the couple wear. "Well, I'm here to let you know that even today, ole Mr. Dinsmoor is unhappy about the town elders censoring his work, but somehow they must have persuaded him, for the sake of the young, because he came out here and did indeed cement over the genitalia."

The man in white Reeboks switches back to his old glasses and gets right up next to Adam's loincloth for a look-see; his buddy microscopes Eve, examining her cement, too. After they're done, Harvey moves in and carefully verifies the fact for himself. He seems absolutely tickled. And I can't tell if it's the wind or just pure happiness, but his face is flushed red.

By this time Darla has us eating out of her hand. "And now that you've become acquainted with ole Mr. Dinsmoor," she says finally in a stagey voice, gesturing toward a low-slung concrete mausoleum across the way, "how would you like to meet him for yourself?" At this the retirees blanch. But Harvey pipes right up for the first time during the whole tour. "I sure would," he says, and then starts himself across the brown-duff lawn, through a stiff wind, to the mausoleum, followed first by the tour guide and then the retirees, who now seem terrified to be left alone, and finally me.

The mausoleum is a mighty special place, according to Darla. Determined to have his first wife in there with him, Dinsmoor dug her up in the local cemetery and then had her placed in the steel vault with him and encased in cement. The top of the coffin is glass, so everyone can have a look, as do about ten thousand tourists a year.

As Dinsmoor claimed, the coffin is especially designed for Judgment Day, so that on Resurrection morn the concrete lid will fly open and "I will sail out like a locust." He also promised a smile for anyone who pays to see him. Our tour guide fiddles with the lock, can't seem to find the key, and while the retirees nervously shift their weight from foot to foot, Harvey stands rock still, in an expectant trance.

Up until now, I admit I've regarded Dinsmoor as sort of a fuzzy-headed left shoe. But then there's the whole stunt of his death here: his self-assurance of immortality. A near masterstroke, for even now the town of Lucas seems to exist mostly because of Dinsmoor. If he was dismissed and despised by the local folk in life, the economics of his immortality have called for his complete resurrection. And this somewhat chilling moment—the moment of our face-to-face meeting with the old man's corpse—is the macabre pinnacle of the Lucas spectacle.

But Dinsmoor isn't the first. In fact, he would only be one in a long line of dead bodies kept around the world past their various due dates for political, economic, medical, and spiritual reasons. However barbaric-seeming, the preservation and reclamation of human body parts are as ancient as human history. From this century, the most famous reside under glass, in luxury, temperature-controlled mausoleums: Lenin, Mao, Ho Chi Minh, Kim Il Sung, the Mongolian revolutionary hero Sukhe Bator. Even now, in Scottsdale, Arizona, a company known as Alcor houses dozens of dead bodies and heads in deep-freeze, waiting for science to find a cure for death itself. And the idea of collecting bodily souvenirs from the dead certainly didn't begin with Thomas Stoltz Harvey. During the Romantic era of the eighteenth century, hearts were the craze. After his death, Chopin's was taken to Poland. The hearts of Shelley and Byron were cut from their bodies and preserved. And the writer Thomas Hardy had his removed, too, though, when returned to his wife, it was eaten by a dog.

With the rise of science and advances in the medical field, brains became de rigueur. But for some, their acquisition had nothing to do with science. The heads of Franz Joseph Haydn, Pancho Villa, and Emanuel Swedenborg all have simply gone missing, while the brains of John Dillinger and John F. Kennedy, among others, have vanished, too. Other famous body parts have surfaced from time to time: Hitler's skull in Russia, Beethoven's hair as the center of a debate about DNA testing, and Napoleon's penis, which was put up for auction in 1972, but withdrawn after an uproar.

In spirit, the eighteenth-century British philosopher Jeremy Bentham comes closest to Dinsmoor. Bentham wished for his skeleton to be dressed in a black suit and top hat and seated in a chair, assuming the same posture as when he was living. It was Bentham's intention to have his skeleton—along with his "preserved" head—participate in medical lectures and performances as a reminder of just how beautiful a body could be. It was his belief, too, that one day everyone might preserve their corpses in like fashion and so the world would be actively inhabited by both the living and the dead, who could serve as Auto Icons. Unfortunately, a mistake was made in preserving Bentham's head, and according to one account it was "rendered as hard as the skulls of New Zealanders"—a public relations gaffe from which Bentham's intended movement never recovered. In the end, Bentham's head was stolen from University College in London by students from rival King's College, later returned, and to this day it is rumored that his ghost haunts the halls of the college, tapping out "Dapple" on his walking stick.

Standing now before Dinsmoor's cement sarcophagus, I have butterflies in my stomach. Behind this door is everything that we've found a convenient way to deny in our lives—by crating the elderly off to nursing homes, by keeping death at a remove, by rhinoplasty and liposuction—and now we're about to pass over to the other side, to meet the great cement-maker himself, Dinsmoor. Darla finally finagles the lock and the chains clatter to the ground. From behind, the retirees overwhelm Harvey and the tour guide and push in first.

Darla shines her flashlight in the dark, catches the coffin with a bright beam, and the two older men let out a collective gasp, then retreat posthaste, just bolt for the doorway, searching for oxygen.

Harvey sidles right up to Dinsmoor, and peeks down at him, a ravaged black and cream skeleton in his finest haberdashery under glass. Apparently the seal is not airtight, and Dinsmoor has paid a heavy tariff. As ugly as he was in life, he's harder to gaze upon now—even through wincing eyes. At the foot of the sarcophagus is a cement jug containing two gallons of water in case the Boss sends Dinsmoor to hell. When Harvey registers the old maverick, he can barely contain himself, all the suppressed giggles and chuckles of the last half hour burst forth in a peal of laughter.

Harvey doesn't want it to end. He lingers awhile over Dinsmoor, who in his dumbed-face skeletal expression kind of strikes me as duped by death, as if Dinsmoor didn't count on the fact that the faucet of his mouth would be shut, too, with his demise. No, it seems he believed he would forever haunt these grounds, jawing about this or that, tapping his own "Dapple." But, after all, he's just these sad bones; he can offer us no smile. When we leave the mausoleum, Harvey returns to the log cabin to view photographs of Dinsmoor. Is it that he identifies somehow with Dinsmoor? That he is awed by the man's crackpot ambition? Or is it something more primal? That in witnessing the life and death of a man who lived so fully outside of society, but so fully inside some secret fetish, it eases the travail of Harvey's own life? Or at the very least guarantees that he won't be remembered as being quite that nutty?

Outside, Harvey wanders back to Dinsmoor's depiction of the seven sins as seven politicians and bankers and other low-down capitalist vermin. It just so happens that Dinsmoor's most productive years coincided with Einstein's, that from his slightly addled brain came all of this, this vision of humanity, this skewed unified theory of everything, as surely as Einstein attempted to envision his own—and ours.

Later in the car, after we've turned south on the back roads, headed for Dodge City, thirty, forty, even a hundred miles from Lucas, I catch Harvey gazing out the window at all that griddled flat land, his shoulders just perceptively moving up and down, the corners of his mouth turned up, giggling again.

Out here, too, we see a rainbow and come face-to-face with a flash of Harvey's own blighted ambition. "I remember more rainbows in Kansas than any other state," he says, blinking his moist eyes at the brilliant beams of blue and green, orange and yellow. "I used to try to photograph rainbows, but they never turned out."

13 ◆ The Pepper Fork

A confession: Over the last week, at truck stops and drive-throughs, in restaurants and random road encounters, I've kept our little secret, and it's begun to take its toll. There have been moments when I've been alone with the brain—Harvey away to the john or dawdling somewhere—when I've opened up the car trunk and looked in, pinched the cold, silver zipper between my thumb and forefinger, applied just enough pressure to begin the unzip, but then couldn't bring myself to do it. Too much of a violation, an untenable breach in our manly society—one based on the equal sharing of crackers and cookies—even as Harvey covets for himself the gray matter upon which our private Skylarkian democracy is founded. In fact, in all of our days together, he hasn't even pretended to make a motion to show me the brain.

"Dr. Harvey," I finally say straight out, "what are the odds I can have a look at that brain?" A beat passes during which Harvey considers. Given such a blunt question he seems unmoved, and unsurprised. And yet, I've clearly communicated an important feeling: that I consider my first, fleeting glimpse of Einstein's brain, in the bad light of that secret room back in Princeton, as only a beguiling appetizer.

"Way-ell . . . ," he says, and then seems to slip back into deep thought, letting a mile marker pass to prove it. And another and another, until I realize he's given me a little limp hip and forearm shiver, like Albie Booth in the open field at the Yale Bowl. It's the most curious thing. And then, as he has before, the map spread out on his lap, Harvey begins reading the story of America, town names clustered in the regions through which we pass: Otis, Radium, Pawnee Rock, Zook. I don't get the sense that he's reading to me exactly; it's more like someone reading to his kids at bedtime, at first to placate them but then so wrapped up in the words that when he stops an hour later, he finds that everyone has long since passed out.

And yet I'm touched by it. He points out that our Route 56 runs along the Arkansas River, and that if we were to follow it to its terminus we'd be in a place called the Turkey Mountains. He lets me know that we've passed thirty-two miles east of the Barbed Wire Museum in La Crosse and twenty-five miles north of the world's largest hand-dug well, in Greensburg. Harvey isn't without a sense of humor, though it's dry and highly sporadic. In fact, waiting for it is like waiting for a cuckoo to appear on the hour—and realizing that, with this particular clock, the cuckoo only arrives once every six or seven hours. When Harvey locates what's called the Salt Fork of the Arkansas River on the map, he deadpans, "Way-ell, I wonder where they keep the Pepper Fork?"

Rolling with the Ogallala aquifer somewhere under our wheels, and huge cow-uddered clouds overhead, we gain a new appreciation for each other. On the radio: steer calves and heifers for sale, Red Angus bulls, yearlings with good genetics and a quality carcass. And then Bobby Darin singing "Beyond the Sea." Harvey taps a finger on his knee, the brain sloshes in its Tupperware. Beyond the dashboard, the earth unfurls—miles of browned grass and loam. In this happy moment, we could probably drive forever. By twilight, there's a nocturne of warm rain on the roof of the Skylark. We pass a pungent nitrogen plant, itself like a twisted metallic brain. Then a momentary moon through the clouds. Water towers gleam in the silver light like spaceships, telephone poles pass like crucifixes, and grain elevators rise like organ pipes from the plains.

On the outskirts of Dodge City, we pass feed yards and primeval slaughterhouses and can make out dark shapes in the pens, thousands of them—British Whites and Herefords, Charolais and Simmentals and Black Anguses. Occasionally we spot a big, boxy cow comically silhouetted by moonlight, atop a mound of mud rising up in the middle of it all. When we enter Dodge City proper, it's like suddenly being underwater on a fluorescent coral reef. We gallop down the strip, past all kinds of honky-tonk, riding with Wyatt Earp and Bat Masterson, past Boot Hill, where the first gunslingers found their final resting places over stupid poker games and too much rotgut, their crooked white-cross graves a tribute in part to something that Einstein once noted: "Americans are colossally bored." There was a day when huge herds of longhorns were driven along the Santa Fe Trail straight into the Wickedest Little City of the West, and then, from here, the railroad took them east for slaughter. The streets of Dodge City were so full of cattle you couldn't part them with a horse, and so many brothels, well, it was apparently hard to avoid fornication, too.

Today, nearly a third of America's meat comes from southwest Kansas, and the cows ride in trailer trucks called pots, ten thousand head a day rolling right down Wyatt Earp Avenue, right past a cluster of motels, including a place called the Astro Motel, which, after a most delicious slab of fillet at the Cowtown Saloon, is where we bed down for the night. I've never stayed in a motel with an American Owned sign. Equipped with an old television and some nice wood paneling, my room includes an electric-pink flyswatter that reads: You're on Target with Us . . . Kills 25 Percent More Flies.

Leaving the Astro the next morning, I go to return our keys. Sitting behind the front desk is the motel manager, an affable middle-aged man, who is just plain Kansas friendly and seems to live in a little room behind the desk with his wife, a woman with cotton-candy-swirled hair. "Where y'all off to?" he asks. And there's a look in his eyes, too, that says he'd go with us if he could. In the face of so much desire, I somehow completely spill my guts. I tell him that we've got the brain in the trunk, that we're headed to California to show it to Einstein's granddaughter. I tell him that the old man in Room 22, he's the guy who cut the thing out of Einstein's head. The manager stops for a moment, like he's been hit by a punch, and looks at me sideways—as surprised as I am, really—then realizes I'm serious, and tries to be hospitable.

"Einstein, huh? That guy knew something," he says, folding his arms, shifting his weight. "That guy really did have a brain. But I wouldn't have wanted to live with him. You know . . . a little weirdy." He spins his finger in a circle around his ear. "I have a nephew who is kind of a genius, but he hasn't flaked off yet. I met a guy in California who was so smart he couldn't talk. He sure could tell you how to look at the moon, but he couldn't tell you how to tie your shoes."

Later, riding with a pack of eighteen-wheelers making time for Abilene, I think about that conversation, the way I just blurted out our secret as if I'd been holding my breath for a long time or, conversely, ordering a deli sandwich. I think about how easy it was, how good it felt. I wasn't bragging so much as sharing—or releasing. And yet I have no idea whether he believed me or simply humored me to get me out of his lobby, if I appeared as strange to him as the vision beyond our window now: the sky, a cerulean blue; the occasional twisted tree, a Japanese character; the wind a momentary haiku; and quanta of sun pouring down 93 million miles to Earth, through solar cloud and purple space, to light the papery face of Thomas Stoltz Harvey, a man of silence after silence.

It seems we've outrun the weather, as well as the season, for with the ageless, nearly sexual magic of the first hot sun on spectral winter skin, we begin to shed our layers and get woozy on the warmth. We motor through Meade, Kansas, and Harvey, in a state of sudden stimulation, remembers this as the Dalton Gang's hideout. He narrows his eyes as we pass through town, cranes his neck to peer down empty streets, but in a minute it's all over—Jo Mama's Drive-in and Thorsell's Drugstore instantly become fallow wheat fields again as if the whole thing were a mirage—and he falls back in his seat, looking slightly perplexed.

In Liberal—the birthplace of L. Frank Baum, author of *The Wizard of Oz*—we eat at a glassed-in coffin of a restaurant called Mr. Breakfast. Old folks arrive in rusted Ford pickups, chain-smoking, hacking phlegm. Swab runny eggs with Wonder bread toast, gulp mud-water coffee. Looking around—Harvey among the chorfing, anonymous throng—one gets the feeling that this is not a bunch racing to embrace a twenty-first century. One man scratches his crotch, another has bits of egg in his mustache. Meanwhile, Harvey closely observes a fly making the rounds from one meal to the next. What is it that he sees now, watching that fly? And is it something less somehow than if Einstein himself were sitting right here, watching that same fly? Is it that genius is really nothing more than a matter of seeing as simply as possible, that somewhere in this world the image already exists waiting for the camera, or the profound idea already exists waiting for the mind to happen on it? After all, from a falling body Einstein pulled out relativity.

And Harvey's genius? He survives . . . and he has the brain.

In fact, he sits there, calmly, getting *younger*. And the rest of us? We sit in a room so full of smoke it seems we ourselves are smoldering, aging at the speed of cooked eggs, perhaps each of us hoping for something to come along and save us. Why shouldn't Einstein's brain—as much as Christ's foreskin or Buddha's toenail—have its own cadre of committed disciples? And why couldn't they be both scientists and pilgrims? After all, Einstein's brain is one of those rare objects in which science and religion actually meet. "Science without religion is lame," Einstein once said, "religion without science is blind."

What's surprising to me is that, while some researchers seem to have experienced ecstatic awe in the presence of Einstein's brain—for instance, Marian Diamond breathlessly describes her first face-to-face meeting with it as "a tingle, a revelation"—others vociferously reject the idea that it carries any power whatsoever. When I talk to Sandra Witelson, the Canadian researcher, she castigates me for the silly suggestion that the brain might be more than just lobe chunks floating in formaldehyde. "This has nothing to do with religion," she tells me. "It's a purely scientific matter."

But then there's Harvey. While claiming the brain for science, he's also protected it like a relic. Even if on occasion his method of storage (cookie jars, living room mantels) has been unconventional, he seems to have derived some power and insight just from knowing that the brain has always been there, by his side. By not issuing a definitive report on the brain—or at least a statement that there is nothing worth a definitive report—Harvey's also helped to mythologize the brain over these last four decades. Eventually, the waiting and wondering, the sheer weight of gossip and the power of the unknown, which finally is the ultimate power of Einstein's brain, overrides the thing itself. If the brain is invisible to the world, as it is now, then it must reside in the imaginations of a committed few, as something symbolic, like a Communion wafer.

⚛

After eating, we gas down into Oklahoma (through Tyrone, Hooker, Guymon, and Texhoma) and then the Texas Panhandle (edging the Rita Blanca National Grasslands, through Stratford, Dalhart, and Romero)—all of it flat, with oil rigs ticking like metronomes. I've taken to photographing Harvey by various signs and monuments along the road, have snapped him at the Garden of Eden, good sport that he is, standing before a cement depiction of the seven sins—lust hovering over his right shoulder, avarice over his left—or the Astro Motel with its American Owned sign, and when we drift by a huge wooden cowboy gunslinger with a Wesson blazing out across the empty plains, Harvey poses between his legs. For the longest time after our trip, after my life has returned to some semblance of normality, I'll keep these same photographs pinned to a wall above my desk as tiny parables.

By the New Mexico border, the wood-frame farmhouses have transmogrified into adobe. We pass an emu farm with a sign out front that says *America's New White Meat*. But seeing those spindly things pecking one another . . . well, I doubt it. In Tucumcari, almost on cue, there's red dirt and tumbleweed. We drive through ruts and washes, over tableland and mesa. Here the hills are testicular, the ancient mounds monslike, but all of it seems dead and washed-out, a monument to its former fecundity and a time when, according to our friend Wayne, this place was overrun by "big fucking dinos."

At one point we pass a gold Caddy shipwrecked on the shoulder, glowing like El Dorado in a blaze of sun. We slow down just as a trooper approaches from the opposite direction; through the car's open front window is a woman with her head thrown back, apparently sleeping off a drunk, or perhaps something worse. The trooper waves us past and so we keep on. But then that woman with long, knotted brown hair, kind of looking like Janis Joplin, with her jagged mouth and pallid skin, with whatever abandon has led her to the breakdown lane somewhere in east New Mexico, she stays with me, takes her place in the constellation of images gathered from the road, and revisits me months later in the most unexpected moments.

With the rush of cacti, and the soft crib-lull of the Skylark, I must admit that my frustration with Harvey's protective zeal about the brain has bled into a kind of benevolent respect, a sudden idea that Harvey actually may be a revolutionary hero. For wasn't he the one who thumbed his nose at everyone, and legged it out West on an end around with the brain? Maybe he thought he was protecting it from the so-called experts, or saving the brain of one of the world's greatest alleged pacifists from the clutches of the U.S. military. "I'm certain it would be lost and forgotten—like so many other famous brains—if it weren't for him," says Elliot Krauss, the man who now holds Harvey's old pathologist position at Princeton Hospital. "No one would have cared for it the way he has. I think history will be very kind to Tom Harvey." And, then, doesn't Harvey's defiance make him the perfect Einsteinian hero?

Maybe, if Harvey knew nothing else, he knew enough to make sure that Einstein's brain didn't get sucked into the maw of the system.

We zag through saguaro and scrub, in the shadow of the Jemez Mountains. I glance at the old man, and see he has momentarily nodded off for the first time all trip, riding on the happy currents of some faraway Pepper Fork. I've sort of nodded off, too. On a straightaway, I look at the speedometer: We're going 115 miles an hour.

14 ◆ What We Talk About When We Talk About Meat

A random thought occurs to me as we speed through New Mexico, as I steal peeks at Harvey's unguarded sleeping self, a face that betrays absolutely nothing: Perhaps I've already met Harvey's alter ego in a place far from here. His name is Kenji Sugimoto and he lives in Japan. Before going cross-country with Harvey, I travel through space and time to visit him in Osaka.

Granted, it's a long way to go to meet an obscure math professor at a place called Kinki University, but Sugimoto is also one of the most prolific collectors of Einsteiniana in the world. And he is among those who believe Einstein's brain is a relic. When I find him at his office at Kinki, he's wearing a green tie with Einstein's face on it. Brown-flowered tea stains bloom on his white shirt. A sock on one foot is inside out. And his hair is frizzed and whipped up in a wild Einstein-like salad.

On Sugimoto's desk is a pack of Omar Sharif cigarettes, absently tossed next to an electric typewriter. He offers me a seat, then realizes it's occupied by a huge canvas, a crude though heartfelt portrait of Einstein in later life. The nose doesn't seem right, more Karl Malden than Albert Einstein—but it was offered to him by one of his students. He briefly admires it by way of registering its importance and sets it on the floor next to a trembling tower of Einstein books. He produces a cache of black-and-white photographs marking Einstein's progress through Japan during his 1922 trip here.

It was a heady, heady time. While Einstein was on a boat from Shanghai to Japan, as part of a five-month trip that included fan-crazed stops in Singapore, Hong Kong, Palestine, and Spain, news came that he had won the Nobel prize. What seemed to make him happiest wasn't the award itself, nor the cash prize ($32,000 that went to his first wife, Mileva, as part of their divorce settlement), but rather a letter of congratulations from his good friend Niels Bohr. The next time the two scientists met in Copenhagen they became so lost in debate over quantum mechanics that they spent hours together on a trolley, traveling to and fro, the neat, fastidious Dane and the German who looked as if he'd just smoked an exploding cigar, absently missing their stop with each new pass.

In Japan, Einstein lectured to packed houses, in one instance speaking through a translator before two thousand people, pontificating for almost six hours on relativity. One theory about Einstein's popularity lay in a bit of confusion: the Japanese characters for "relativity principle" were quite similar to those for "love" and "sex," and so apparently some felt that a shaggy Tantric guru had landed in their midst. Upon meeting him, one Japanese man, assuming Einstein was not a scientist at all but a holy visionary, was awed by how the schlumpy German, someone who looked quite the opposite of an angel, could so accurately see into God's heaven. "He has a quiet way of walking," wrote a Japanese cartoonist, Ippei Okamoto, who traveled with the Einsteins, "as if he is afraid of alarming the truth and frightening it away."

In Kenji's hand now are photographs taken during Einstein's visit to Osaka. These are among his most prized possessions: Einstein wearing a heavy overcoat and wide-brim hat against the December chill, looking more exorcist than physicist. Einstein jamming on a piano. Einstein standing before a chalkboard scrawled with inscrutable equations, a nimbus of numbers about his head, under the rapt gaze of his audience.

As we riffle through the photographs, the professor runs his fingers over them as if reading braille, traces the path on which Einstein is seen walking, gently touches the great scientist's head. His eyes turn watery staring at a photo of Einstein later in life, when the weight of age has driven him earthward, when he only has several years left to live. "I wanted to meet Albert Einstein, but he died when I was eight years," says Kenji, who grew up in Nagasaki after the war. "When I meet Albert Einstein's brain, I meet Einstein."

We're interrupted by a knock at the door—three sharp raps—and then in step the polished wingtips of a man introduced to me only as Abe, Kenji's good friend and secretary of the Einstein World Congress, an organization founded by Sugimoto to further cooperation among Einstein scholars and enthusiasts, as well as to establish the first-ever Albert Einstein museum. Abe is dressed in a very sharp, sheeny suit the color of the sea off Bora Bora. Sugimoto and Abe stand amid the clutter—in the blown-up wreckage of Sugimoto's office—talking turkey. They need $3 million to make the museum work, and most of all they need the support of the powerful Mr. Kobe, the director of Kinki University and the man who apparently can make it rain gold doubloons if he likes the cut of your jib. Abe is here to join us for lunch with the powerful Mr. Kobe and, when Sugimoto consults his wristwatch and realizes we're late, both World Congress members suddenly look stricken, compose themselves, straighten their respective ties, slap each other on the back as a kind of psych, then lead me out of the office and up the elevator.

When I first spy the powerful Mr. Kobe, he is sitting behind a large desk, chatting on the phone. He is a larger man than either Sugimoto or Abe, with big hands and an impassive face. He has a way of looking through a person, to the skeleton reality of who you really are. He gives me a grave look and a bone-crushing handshake. I'm introduced as an American scholar, though he doesn't even pretend to buy that nonsense. In his presence even Sugimoto is more subdued, a bit more manly. There's some tough-guy small talk, and the powerful

Mr. Kobe's voice is a low, commanding rumble like a tank unit running through an abandoned village. Everything rides behind it.

Lunch is a seaweed salad and steaming bowls of udon, plates of godai and some wobbly gelatin concoction that even Kenji avoids, though the powerful Mr. Kobe sucks his down in one emphatic swallow. With the food, the mood lightens. Abe lays out a business plan for the Einstein museum and Sugimoto breaks in every now and again with a statement, uttered seriously, that seems utterly unserious. With each intervention the powerful Mr. Kobe lets out a low Lurch-like growl as if stricken by indigestion, then goes back to chain-smoking. The Einstein congressmen take this as a good sign—and it does seem to be one! Even now, when the powerful Mr. Kobe gazes out at the Kusunoki Mountains, he seems to be considering the cost-benefit, neon-light proposition of Kinki University's Einstein museum, a place where day and night the citizens of the world will stand on line, pockets bursting with yen.

"Einstein give Mr. Kobe happy feeling," Sugimoto says to me when we leave his office, though it's unclear that any real business has been done. And then suddenly Sugimoto is chugging and puffing past the university gates, swimming through the streets, past electronics stores and office buildings, toward a woman on the horizon now, a beautiful woman wearing an Annie Hall hat pulled down to her eyes. She is lithe and small-boned, a continent unto herself, fitting neatly between the ice floes of human traffic in a long, funky brown dress with velvet trimmings, neither waiting nor unwaiting, just there, in a yoga afterglow. Her hair streams down around a silver planet pendant she wears, some kind of metallic Mercury, and she is smiling. A beatific smile as if she stands on the threshold between the visible and invisible worlds, more radiant and alive than other breathing creatures, which makes her impossible to miss.

And yet Kenji blows right by her. Lost in thought. Lost in dialogue with the Great One. Ten yards past, he stops and snaps his fingers.

"Einstein move my feet," he says with a bashful smile, "right past my wife." Her name is Sami and she, too, falls in behind Kenji, who is now leading us to Kompon Dai-to, or the Fundamental Great Pagoda, the place where Einstein himself visited sixty-five years ago. An immense vermilion and white structure, it houses a statue of Dainichi Nyorai, the cosmic or solar Buddha of esoteric Buddhism.

It's like this with Kenji Sugimoto: You don't know where you're going until you're there.

We roam the pagoda, then Sugimoto takes off again at breakneck speed through the adjoining park, stops near a man selling wafers to feed the deer that roam the park, sniffs the air, and turns back to us and declares, "Einstein come here!" Then he is off again, in an arbor of cherry trees, revolving, head craned upward to the branches. He looks quizzically back down the walking lane from where we just came, sizes up the scene, and blurts, "Ah-so, Einstein here!"

Sami and I lumber to keep up, and Sami admits that this kind of behavior once troubled her, twenty-five years ago when they first married. "I became jealous," she says in excellent English, as Kenji makes a beeline for a pile of leaves. "I thought I married one man and then suddenly there were three of us." What Sami realized was that her husband had a doppelganger: Einstein. And there were so many uncanny parallels between the two. Both failed important exams during university; both floundered trying to find jobs once they'd graduated. And while Kenji simply felt lost, Einstein's adversities seemed to rise out of a swaggering cocksureness about his own genius and were caused in part by the way he humiliated his teachers for their comparative ignorance.

By comparison, Kenji, who is forty-six years old, has yet to discover any major new principle about the universe, though he claims it is only a matter of time. And why not? As much as any dark horse, why not Professor Kenji Sugimoto? When we get back to Kinki University, Kenji seats both Sami and me on a Naugahyde couch in the teachers' lounge, then rushes from the room and returns with a videotape, the BBC documentary made by Kevin Hull, the filmmaker I met in London, about Kenji's journey to America to find Dr. Harvey and Einstein's brain. Kenji refers to it as "my movie." In it, he criss-crosses the country on a bizarre, month-long odyssey from the corridors of Princeton Hospital to a succession of humdrum mid-western towns, dogging anyone who might know anything about Einstein's brain until he finds Dr. Harvey in Lawrence, Kansas, an old man sleeping on a sofa bed in a cramped apartment. When Kenji requests a piece of Einstein's brain, Harvey takes a steak knife from a kitchen drawer, places his hand in a glass cookie jar full of brain, and fishes out a slab, plopping it on a wood cutting board, where he silently begins slicing.

It's an utterly strange and wonderful moment; buoyed by unbridled joy, Kenji literally bear-hugs Harvey from behind, latches on to the old man's stomach, rests his oversized head against the back of Harvey's own small bird skull, and won't let go. While Sami and I watch—Sami laughing uncontrollably—Kenji buzzes in and out of the teachers' lounge, barely able to contain himself. Onscreen he grumbles and grunts. Offscreen, he emits the same primal, snorty sounds of porcine rummagings through sludge and orange peels.

In Hull's film, which is Sugimoto's film ("I am Kenji Sugimoto," says Hull. "We are all Kenji Sugimoto"), the pilgrim, like all pilgrims, has necessarily traveled many hard miles through a foreign land; he has suffered GI upset from stale morning Danish clipped from the lobbies of an endless progression of Days Inns. His body has grown heavy in order for his soul to soar. And now the onscreen Kenji, presented with a slice of Einstein's brain, is simply overcome. He is Mr. Whipple uncontrollably squeezing the Charmin; he's the gourmand carnivore served the perfect filet mignon; he's arrived in Mecca for the hajj, making seven awestruck, counterclockwise rings around the Ka'bah.

And it is here where the off-screen Kenji, the real Kenji, intervenes. Impatiently, emphatically, he plunks a white canister on the table before Sami and myself, switching off the television, then pacing around the table a couple of times. Then he rolls up his sleeves, loosens the knot of his tie, and unlids it. Inside the canister is a tea tin, a purple Twinings container (flavor: Lapsang Souchong Te). Kenji gently removes it and again pries off another lid. Here he reaches slowly into its dark gullet and pulls out two widemouthed, plastic pill containers. These he ceremoniously sets on the table, as if he's handling two Fabergé eggs.

When he screws off these last lids, we both draw close, expectantly. "Einstein brain," says Kenji, beaming broadly, gesturing to the formaldehyde pools in each container. The smell catches me first; Sami just leans back, closing her eyes, looking seasick. I come forward, breathing solely through my mouth. What floats in the liquid looks less like a brain than a sneeze. Just gobby pieces of phlegm. "*Shono*," Kenji blurts, in his excitement momentarily abandoning his English. Cerebellum. Shaped like a bonsai tree. "Piece of Einstein's brain bring harmony," he says. "My spirit belong to Einstein's brain." He pages through a Japanese-English dictionary that he has brought with him from his office. "*Shugo*," he says. Divine protection. Then: "*Ishiki*." Consciousness, one's self. We sit in silence, and after a time, I move closer to the floating brain bits again. "*Omamori*," Kenji says. A charm, a talisman.

His belief is an all-consuming, humbling thing. "But what does it mean?" I ask him, both repulsed and fascinated. Kenji furrows his brow, starts to speak, then stops, then starts again, considers the question at length, trying to forge the perfect grammatical sentence. "To be or not to be," he says. "This is what Einstein's brain is all about."

After seeing the brain, there is nothing to do but celebrate by going to a karaoke lounge, a favorite haunt of Kenji and his colleagues. There are seven or eight "ladies" who attend to the clientele, a collection of suited men in various states of besotment. I'm introduced to Miss Michiko Miyata, the matron of the lounge, a short, friendly, overbusy woman who employs a quiet arsenal of hand signals, whispers, rib prodding, and foot stamping, all with a smile, to keep her girls in line and on the ready. The hostesses have names like Jun and Kyoko and one nineteen-year-old Chinese singer with oeil-de-boeuf eyes of soft brown liquid is called Lily.

Of all people, the powerful Mr. Kobe is here, too, wearing his Noh mask of no expression, sitting in a dark corner, accepting visits from his minions, chain-smoking Omar Sharif cigarettes and making neat work of his scotch. He is here, I'm told, six nights a week, all except Sunday. And I'm told that it is my obligation, when summoned, to sit with him for a short while. When I'm indeed called forth from my table, Sami accompanies me for the purpose of translation, while Kenji is lost deep in song with one of the hostesses, swaying in a trance, reading lyrics off a big screen.

The powerful Mr. Kobe regards me from behind a wraith of smoke but shows no flicker of recognition. The set of his face is severe, a perpetual frown from the heavy, heavy weight of his world. Then, in the gravelly Panzer rumble of his voice, he fires a few questions at me about America, about free trade, about how I regard Japan. He peppers me with a few more about his university, its comparison to those of the Ivy League. And yet my answers seem to mean nothing; no, it's the questions that matter. Or the drama of the questions. The long Bogart drag on his cigarette, the expiration of tobacco, the slow movement of the powerful Mr. Kobe's martial hand toward a porcelain tray to chip off the ash. It's with a grunt that I'm suddenly dismissed, and some other poor yabbler fills my seat.

One of the most pleasant surprises of the night is that Sugimoto has a beautiful, Wayne Newton voice, a supple manliness in the notes he sings to a syrupy Japanese favorite, "Blue Airport," the tale of two lovers separated by a plane trip of some sort, thankfully reunited when the return ticket is executed. He sways; he closes a fist to show pain. And so the songs are sung, Kenji dueting with everyone, or just bellowing on his own, pouring his soul out to a room full of lost, cross-eyed men.

After some point in the evening, everyone is sloshed and beginning on a maudlin march to some unknown destination. Sami sits next to me, hands in her lap, smiling. Whatever discomfort she might feel in coming face-to-face with the geisha girls of Kenji's every karaoke night, she shows no trace of it; in fact, she seems interested in each utterance of these waiting women armed with their lighters and warm towels. As the night has progressed the hostess named Lily has sung with a slew of men, and now Sami tells me that this is Lily's last evening with the troops after three years of singing at this lounge, of being in all of their lives. She is going back to China in the morning.

It is very late when, at the urging of the patrons, Lily picks up one of the cordless mikes and begins a slow, sad good-bye song in Chinese. She is unquestionably stunning—long black hair, full lips, a thin back partially revealed by her gown. As she sweetly finds the notes, as she throws herself into one last song, I realize people are weeping. The hostesses. The men. Sami. And Lily, who has been doing just fine, begins to falter, realizes that this is it, that her life lived at night in the cozy confines of this pink-lit lounge, among so many men who have become like fathers to her, among her fellow sisters who have watched her become a woman, this life of money and freedom and joy will so cruelly end with a short flight to Beijing and the prison of her family.

And then she is blubbering, honest wails that she tries to suppress, her grief monstrously revealed in the professional spotlight. The music carries on without her, mournfully, slowly, but with a trace of seeming malice now. Though she is trying not to lose face, she can only eke out a word or two of each verse in an attempt to catch up, bent at the waist, covering her eyes. In her last act as a karaoke lounge singer, she is dying onstage. Suddenly, a wave of discomfort washes over the room. Oh, how could it be? Embarrassment! But then, suddenly, just as one hostess begins to rush toward the crumpled girl, a voice rises out of nowhere like a large-winged bird, out of the shadows in the room, on a second cordless mike. A strong full-timbred voice, deep and sure, conveying with each note the ache and pathos of good-bye, the rent feelings of everyone in the room, the death of this era, the Lily years. There is such emotion in it, a remarkable lifetime of feeling, really, and yet such strength that even Lily looks up from where she is kneeling, a single tear sparkling on her cheek. And rising from his table, stepping into the spotlight is—impossible—the powerful Mr. Kobe.

He is a towering, awesome presence. And who knew he could speak Chinese? He stands before Lily in his well-tailored suit, though he doesn't offer her a hand. He just sings. Lily, looking up to him, gains her balance, rises from the floor, and begins to sing again, too, and he carries her right to the end. And everybody—including Kenji—is bawling. When the song is over, Lily smiles, then turns to the powerful Mr. Kobe and bows to him. He nods stiffly, retires to his table, and then later, when she visits him one last time, sitting in the visitor's chair, he presents her with an envelope full of money. Even as formality and reticence slowly reassert themselves, something has happened here that no one will forget. It's one of the most honest acts of love I've ever witnessed.

Out in the early-morning street again, six of us pile into a cab— Kenji, Sami, me, and three of their inebriated friends. No one says anything. We just watch as the neon lights of downtown Osaka fall into the melancholy swirl of the river. Exhausted and empty, but pressed together. During the war, after Tokyo was firebombed, American fighter jets attacked Osaka, destroying much of the downtown where we now drive. Kenji himself was born in the short years after his own hometown, Nagasaki, was obliterated. His parents somehow survived the horrors of Einstein's most dubious legacy: the bomb.

It's only when we come to where I'm staying, only after I've gotten out of the cab and placed a hand on its closed door, that Kenji comes down from some faraway place in his mind. "To be, Mr. Michael," he says. "It's much better *to be.*"

15 ✦ I Am the Leg of You

The road has lulled us into a fugue state. Without being fully aware of it, we've become a little shorter of breath and a little dizzier, too, on this gradual climb to eight thousand feet, up through Santa Fe, then northwest, gripped to the switchbacks along the crags that rim Pajarito Plateau, to Los Alamos. Before the Second World War, this was just Indian wasteland. But sometime after Einstein's letter to President Roosevelt pressing for the construction of an atomic bomb, the Defense Department commandeered this middle-of-nowhere. The Los Alamos scientists and staff lived behind barbed wire, were known by number rather than name, and received all correspondences through one post office box in Santa Fe—Box 1663. The bomb was simply referred to as "the gadget." And time was measured in dead bodies, for by the Alamosans' equation, every day of delay in building an atomic weapon meant that more Americans would die at war.

Driving into town, the barracks and mud streets of the 1940s have given way to bland western subdivisions and American prosperity. We pass a spiffy natatorium. We pass nice faux-adobe homes and, in the way that everything connects, the site of a former boys' school that William Burroughs himself once attended. We pass high, electrified fences behind which America's latest weapons research now occurs. Where the U.S. government will soon discover that someone has been siphoning classified information to China for years.

By the gravity of his gaze Harvey leaves the impression that history is being made by his own visit—and that of Einstein's brain. After all, thanks to his letter to FDR, Albert Einstein is inadvertently one of the founding fathers of the Town That Never Was. And now part of the great scientist has arrived here—if fifty-something years late—cruising toward the Bradbury Science Museum.

The museum is a modest, three-room pavilion walled with text and grainy black-and-white photographs that detail the scientific as well as human challenges of building the bomb, while lionizing the patriotic men and women who contributed to the Manhattan Project, most especially its director Robert Oppenheimer. Sure enough, the first exhibit is a photograph of Einstein, and then a copy of his letter to President Roosevelt, behind glass. Harvey stands before it, reading, nodding seriously, then moves on. There's no mention of Einstein's regret at having written the letter. Instead, with a little selective editing, the museum, the town, the feat of dropping two bombs, comes with an Einsteinian seal of approval. The museum—and the culture of Los Alamos as a whole—is most glaringly defined by what its curators seem to have forgotten about the bomb.

What isn't shown here is an August 1945 morning in central Hiroshima, trolleys packed with civilians, thousands of schoolgirls in the streets. The museum doesn't show the B-29, the *Enola Gay,* with pilot Paul Tibbets at the controls, drifting above at 31,000 feet, then releasing four tons of metal through the air, Little Boy. Or the side of the bomb with its autographs and obscene messages (one starts, "Greetings to the Emperor . . .") and emblazoned with the crude naked likeness of Rita Hayworth. What is forgotten are the forty-three seconds of utter silence, the time it takes Little Boy to drop on the city, and then a blast that equals 12,500 tons of TNT. And then the horrific vision at ground zero, at the Aioi Bridge: birds incinerating in the air, people flaming like candles and swelling like bronze Buddhas. And this is just the beginning.

The museum doesn't show the firestorm that soon pulverizes the city, the atomic winds that whip into a tornado. The nine out of every ten bodies dead within a mile of the blast, the 200,000 people who will finally be counted dead, and the sticky black rain carrying radioactive fallout that beats relentlessly down on the survivors. It doesn't show people with skin hanging from their bodies like kimonos. Afterward, it doesn't show Nagasaki and the 140,000 more Japanese civilians who will die in like fashion. One can spend hours in the museum—as Harvey does, finally exiting exhilarated by the amazing ingenuity of science—but the devastation remains invisible.

So, what part did Einstein really play in this? The abiding impression of Einstein—one propagated by his handlers after his death—was essentially that of a pacifist for every season. "I appeal to all men and women," he wrote in a 1931 statement to the War Resisters International, "to declare that they will refuse to give any further assistance to war or the preparation of war." And in a later letter to a magazine editor, he put a finer point on his own personal feelings: "My pacifism is an instinctive feeling, a feeling that possesses me because the murder of people is disgusting. My attitude is not derived from any intellectual theory but is based on my deepest antipathy to every kind of cruelty and hatred."

And yet it's understandable that the Nazis, with their concentration camps full of Jews, would have provoked him. During the war years, too, the American mind-set boiled down to the ultimate zero-sum: destroy and win or be destroyed and lose. Thus, Einstein's famous letter to FDR advocating the building of an atomic weapon is something that, while paradoxical, is at least explainable. And of course, later, in conversation with Linus Pauling, he recanted that letter. But was Einstein merely burnishing his sainthood by articulating regret? Did pacifism only suit him when it seemed to suit him best?

What's surprising is that beneath the great scientist's holy veneer of pacifism, Einstein was more involved in the American war cause than most people think, a fact first brought to light by the Einstein biographer Ronald Clark. Even as Hoover and his agents tirelessly collected evidence against "the extreme radical," right up until the scientist's death, Einstein was intermittently employed by U.S. Navy's Bureau of Ordnance as a scientist, technician, and explosives consultant. Among the host of projects on which he worked, he helped evaluate American plans to mine and attack a Japanese naval base.

When I later go to check the Einstein file at the National Archives in College Park, Maryland, after our road trip, I happen upon a number of letters that Einstein wrote to the Bureau's Lt. Stephen Brunauer. After passing through security at the Archives—which are housed in a new glass and steel building—I'm taken to a vast reading room where accordion files are delivered to me by John Taylor, a wizened, hunched man with a courtly southern drawl. About eighty years old, he's been working at the Archives since World War II. The old man happily tells me he'll do what he can to "get the goods" for me—whatever that means—then disappears.

After an hour or so, Taylor reappears with a single folder, marked RG 74. And there they are: nine typed letters addressed to Lt. Stephen Brunauer, all between June 1943 and October 1944, as well as several pages written in Einstein's cramped, neat hand. At first, the letters confuse me, for after reading through so much FBI-generated propaganda bashing Einstein as an enemy of the state, it seems impossible that the Navy would have had anything to do with him. But it gladly did. Some of the letters include sketches made by Einstein of torpedoes and torpedo heads, triggering devices and equations attempting to figure out the best way to create the most effective possible detonation beneath the armored hull of an enemy ship.

"It seems to be desirable to have a device which automatically brings to explosion a torpedo passing below a ship at the right moment," he writes in one letter. "I have an idea for an electro-magnetic device for this purpose which I would like to submit to you for your judgement." In another, the man who fled Germany as a youth to avoid military service, who was spooked by the goon mentality of the armed forces, refers to "my Navy appointment" and then, in another, to "financial matters." In addition, Einstein seems to have met often with Navy officials at 112 Mercer Street.

On the one hand, it's startling to imagine that Einstein would have allowed himself to be so used—even given his antipathy for the Germans. And then there's the deeper troublement of Einstein using his brain toward some military end, for reading these letters somehow makes it easier to imagine Einstein's brain today, cloned and set again on matters of annihilation. And then the letters are also dismaying for the shadow that they cast over Einstein's pacifist proclamations. After all, the great pacifists of our time proved their points by endurance and faith, by not changing their minds, and often by paying the ultimate physical price. What credibility would Gandhi have had if he spent his free time doodling torpedoes or trying to figure out how to up the kill rate on a detonation?

Einstein must have been troubled, too, because he later went into denial about his participation in the war effort. Responding to questions about the atomic bomb in 1952, Einstein told a reporter, "You are mistaken in regarding me as a kind of chieftain of those scientists who abuse science for military purposes. I have never worked in the field of applied science, let alone for the military. I condemn the military mentality of our time just as you do. Indeed, I have been a pacifist all of my life and regard Gandhi as the only truly great political figure of our age."

The difference, of course, is that Einstein wasn't a political leader, though he avidly offered his political opinions again and again in hopes of changing a world he often saw as barbaric. Nonetheless, I can't help but think that, if Los Alamos was America's secret, then maybe these nine letters were Einstein's. Beyond his philandering— which he didn't care to hide—the letters say something more detrimental about Einstein. For in his emphasis on an impersonal universe, he seemed to have constructed a defense for his own retreat from those people who loved him, the same ones he mistreated most. Oddly, he once commended his son Hans Albert—with whom he had no real relationship and whose birthday he never remembered— for having the same outlook. "It is a joy for me to have a son who has inherited the main trait of my personality: the ability to rise above mere existence by sacrificing oneself through the years for an impersonal goal," he wrote a year before his death. "This is the best, indeed the only way in which we can make ourselves independent from personal fate and from other human beings."

But then, why reject human beings as well as the idea that your fate may be inextricably bound to them? If we live in an impersonal universe, in which the accomplishment of impersonal goals (an exploding torpedo, a unified theory, the dropping of an atomic bomb) becomes life's purpose, then what about the human beings? When Paul Tibbets, the pilot of the *Enola Gay*, was asked to justify the killing of 200,000 people at Hiroshima, he simply responded, "It all seemed so impersonal."

Sitting in the reading room that day at the Archives, sifting through those letters, I remember feeling piqued—and then a bit betrayed, the same way I feel now, on this day at Los Alamos, as Harvey's reverence for the crack team of bygone American scientists working round-the-clock on the Manhattan Project, his awe at their gutsiness, obscures what they really accomplished, half a world away, in Kenji Sugimoto's Japan, in Kenji Sugimoto's own birthplace of Nagasaki.

⚛

We spend the night at the ranch of some good friends of mine near Cerrillos, a surly little pit stop whose claim to fame is the fact that Hollywood has filmed several Westerns in its dirt streets. We peel off on a rutted road just south of town, run along an arroyo, and then curl back into a stunning, hundred-acre valley where my friends Clare and Scott live on a ranch once owned by Clare's mother. Both in their thirties, both refugees from San Francisco, the two met at a yoga retreat, and kept up a long-distance relationship for several years, as Scott, a financial whiz, moved to London and Chicago for jobs, and Clare, a P.R. whiz, worked seven days a week and traveled around the world for her own job. When Clare's mother, a painter whose canvases adorn the walls of the house, died of cancer, Clare and Scott quit their jobs and moved here, to the place where she was most present, to make a new life together.

The best thing is that their new life includes so many cats, dogs, horses, and chickens—and each with such exquisite names (Santo, Confiado, Mismo, Guapo, Mono, Paloma, and Houdini)—that two road-weary humans arriving for the night hardly represent a blip on the radar. The main house is made of adobe with several kivas, which are lit with fires. On the fridge is magnetic poetry, a refreshing change from psychopathic rantings scrawled in cross-country men's rooms. I stand for a minute, studying the fridge and its piecemeal poetry. Behind me, the fire crackles and the sweet smell of cedar fills the house. I realize I've forgotten how very simple a little straight-up love can be: "I am the leg of you," reads one line.

Harvey takes an immediate shine to Clare—and Scott, too. Who wouldn't? A pretty, smallish woman with green cat eyes, Clare is the kind of absolutely cheerful person with whom you're instantly on intimate terms. And Scott has a head full of springy hair, a rock climber's body, and an uncensored mouth. He's all yang to Clare's yin.

Since everyone's getting on so well, I excuse myself to do some laundry, my first unfettered time away from Harvey. It feels powerfully good to drop the dirty stuff of a long week into a tub of sudsy water and have my pants and shirts come out clean. I go outside and begin an archaeological dig, cleaning out the car, and it's like a second life. I go for a run, sucking that pure New Mexico air and I feel as if I'm floating up off the earth.

For dinner we drive to a restaurant in town. Over pork tenderloin smeared with chipotle sauce, Clare and Scott finally can't contain themselves.

"I hope you won't find this too forward," Clare says to Harvey, "but I was wondering about your interesting friend. . . ."

"And she's definitely not talking about *him*," says Scott, pointing at me. Then: "We've got a few questions about Einstein's brain."

Harvey blushes, pleased. Fired on shiraz—every time the bottle goes empty, Clare orders another—Harvey becomes downright animated. "Way-ell," he says, dabbing a napkin at the side of his mouth. "I can try to answer them for you."

"Did you ever meet Einstein, you know, before the brain?" asks Scott.

"Yes, I did," says Harvey. "Took blood from him."

Scott considers, scratches his head. "Then remind me to never have you take *my* blood," he blurts, and starts cracking up. Clare giggles, and Harvey . . . Harvey busts a gut. He laughs until he's medium rare.

"Was he friendly?" asks Clare.

"Wore khakis and boat shoes, real comfortable dresser," says Harvey. "I'd say he was extremely friendly. . . ."

"So friendly that he just decided to give you his brain?" asks Scott.

"Hmmm . . . yes and no. He bequeathed it to science and I was lucky to be there that day."

"So you were Science," says Clare.

"Way-ell, never thought about it like that, but I guess so. I took the brain out at the autopsy."

Harvey tells them about how he struck a deal with Hans Albert to publish the findings of his study in a medical journal. "You see, there's an awful lot of interesting information showing up in the research," he says. "It's not just another brain, after all." He describes fixing the brain and admits that his one mistake was injecting it with warm formaldehyde instead of cold formaldehyde, thus hastening its

denaturation. He describes photographing it, slicing it, and number-
ing the slices. Clare and Scott sit rapt. Meanwhile, I glance over my
shoulder to see if anyone is tuned to our conversation. To be honest,
with all this talk of brain, I'm having a hard time eating. "It's a real
tray-sure," Harvey says. "I've gotten to meet many famous people,
many who knew Einstein."

When we return to the ranch, everyone settles by the fire with
mugs of steaming tea. I steal another moment away from the group,
time I've coveted on this day before moving into the last leg of our
journey. I fold laundry and then try to call Sara. When she doesn't
answer, I'm hit with a powerful wave of homesickness. The feeling of
oneness here, the way our friends have decided to live a life together,
to retreat from the mania of their former selves as globe-trotting pro-
fessionals and instead make this wonderland of animals—all of it
spills out as possibility and hope, as another dimension beyond dis-
illusionment. I leave a message, with one of their cats climbing on my
shoulder and an iguana staring at me from the windowsill: "I'm a
prisoner of this zoo until you call." Then I doze off.

When I wake an hour later, Harvey and Clare are alone at the dining table, flushed with excitement. They lower their voices when I
come in. When I leave the room again, they raise them right on cue
and start twittering. Clare is smitten. And Harvey has that Dinsmoor
twinkle about him. Later, I pull Clare aside, to ask some questions:
What's Harvey's magic? Does the brain turn her on? Does she feel
hypnotized? "He's a very, very interesting man," she says. "And for
some men chivalry is not dead. Did you see him pull out my chair for
me before dinner?"

Scott doesn't mind the flirtation, in fact seems satisfied by it
somehow. Before bed, he rallies everyone for a hot tub. I'm confi-
dent that Harvey will sit this one out, but of course he doesn't.
Shambles out in a borrowed bathrobe and baggy swim trunks, dips
a toe in the boiling water. It's a pretty chilly night, stars glazed in the
sky like cold coins on black ice. Van Biesbroeck 8, Vega, T Tauri, Beta

Pictoris. Just as I find myself worrying about the physiological ram-
ifications of dropping an eighty-four-year-old body into 104-degree
water, Harvey throws himself in like a heavy stone. "OH, OH, HEH-
HEH. WOW, THAT'S HOT. WOW, WOW, WOW!!!"

We simmer for a while, chitchatting over the bubbler. Scott suggests that, after Harvey finishes his study on Einstein's brain, it would
only be proper to launch it into space on a private rocket where it
could take its rightful place next to Timothy Leary's ashes. Harvey
chuckles at that, and then Clare pipes up.

"Well, it *is* the color of the moon tonight, isn't it?" she says.

Her observation just kind of hangs there for a moment, until I've
computed the following: While I was briefly snoozing, *somebody* got
a look at the brain. Later, I'll find out that Harvey opened the duffel
for both of them, unpeeled the Tupperware top, fingered chunks of
the brain, and then gave a little show-and-tell. But now, I simply
stutter.

"You mean . . ."

"We really didn't want to wake you up," says Clare.

"But . . ." I look at Harvey, who floats with his eyes closed, lost to
the music of the bubbler. This hits me hard. I've driven two thousand
miles—no, I've chauffeured for two thousand miles, I've made
arrangements at hotels and motels, I've escorted the good doctor
through restaurants and museums, I've watched over him like a
bodyguard as we've made our way toward Evelyn Einstein—and not
been allowed so much as a peek at the brain. Meanwhile my friends,
doing nothing but being their friendly selves, got to see it within a
few hours of meeting the old man.

A steely silence descends, and Clare and Scott delicately announce
that they're going to bed. They slip out of the tub and into the house
as if I've suddenly grown gator teeth. Harvey lays in a trance, his pale
body streaming away from him underwater. And I just sit and glare
at him for a while. What can I do? I decide to outlast him as a kind
of revenge, prepare myself for the pleasure of victory when he gets up

to go, imagine some sort of good night: *Oh, I see, too hot for you . . . it's best to be safe.* Something with a little bite to it.

But then I wait for as long as I can take it, really. My fingers begin to wrinkle between the wrinkles. The top of my head feels as if it's been screwed off and loaded with little stars. Neither of us speaks a word. There's only the sound of the wind and the bubbler. And damn if the old man doesn't seem to show a single sign of relenting. Finally, grudgingly, I lift myself from the tub, from its magic eternal spring, and splosh inside, leaving him hammocked in those dark, boiling waters, keening softly with pleasure—*ahhh, play-sure*—alone beneath the frigid cosmos.

The only thing that saves me from utter freefall—from wanting to pack up in the middle of the night and just bid adios to Harvey and Einstein's brain—is a note left on my pillow, on a scrap of paper, in Clare's hand.

Two words: *Sara called.*

16 ◆ Murky Time

We now have our moments, Harvey and I. Little grumpy moments. I don't even pretend to make conversation; he takes wordless solace in the atlas. I neurotically fiddle with the radio; he stares out the window. Later, he will write to a friend about me: "[We] were compatible for the most part, though he had a hard time judging the time it would take us to get to our destination and I saw more of California in the dark than I would have relished."

Where perhaps I imagined something greater unfolding between us, where I've found that I've somehow come to care about the old man, Harvey still gives no indication that he sees me as anything more than his chauffeur. And apparently a chauffeur less worthy of seeing the brain than complete strangers. Which is how this chill has descended between us. We enter what the Norwegians call the dark months of winter: *Morketiden.* Murky time.

Now the interstate is haunted by white crosses that mark the spots of fatal wrecks. Near an overpass on the outskirts of Albuquerque, a pile of flowers memorializes one family—a mother and her two children—who were killed on a recent Christmas eve by a Navajo man who came roaring down the wrong side of the highway, drunk, and collided head-on with their station wagon. On the highway's shoulder, too, we begin to see more and more hitchhikers, wearing beaten expressions, in fatigue jackets or ripped shirts, an underground railroad of the tattered homeless spooking the road west in hopes of more warmth and better luck. Their faces are the same sienna color as the earth.

Through reservation lands and onto Arizona, a radio station blurs in and out with an oddly familiar, quavering voice. "Satan, I command thee . . . OUT!" It's Bob Larson, the televangelist from the motel room in Kansas, performing an exorcism. And that voice in all of this emptiness, fighting Beelzebub, causes my throat to tighten. When the station frizzles for a moment, a voice intervenes in Navajo, reading what seem to be Bible scriptures, speaking in tongues. Then Bob Larson again: "I command thee: Beast, come out of her mind and emotion! Come out in the name of Jesus!" There are angels and devils brawling everywhere before us. A tree full of dark crows.

In the vast nothingness of Arizona, running parallel to the highway, a train slivers west in the late-day sun—silver passenger cars and sleeping cars and dining cars glinting coast-to-coast behind two black engines. Were this 1931, Einstein very well might have been on that train, on the last leg of his own cross-country journey to Los Angeles and a visit to Cal Polytechnic. He would have slept on clean white sheets and dined on honeyed ham. He would have told his favorite bawdy jokes and teased everyone mercilessly. In the comfort of his compartment, he might have had a pipe or played his violin. Undoubtedly, he would have occasionally looked up from his equations to see America beyond the window. And perhaps his gaze would have fallen across this tableland right here on a day just like today: sun sinking, sky filling with pink and orange light, great expanses of land just sitting, seemingly waiting for the return of big creatures to make it small again. Would he have felt what I feel? That the farther you travel into the country—past the point in Pennsylvania where mountains flatten, past the place in Kansas where trees disappear—the farther you move beyond yourself.

Bathed in the last dopamine rays of the sun, we've reached that moment in the course of every road trip when exhaustion and discombobulation spill into a kind of ecstasy, towns darkly flashing like trout in a river. All things—the strains of "Wild Horses" now on the radio, the galactic motion of driving, the purple night descending—seem like one perfect, unalloyed thing, haunted through. And I'm reminded of Charles Lindbergh, with his four sandwiches and bottle of water, with his ultimate faith in a little 223-horsepower airplane, *Spirit of St. Louis*, up over the Atlantic Ocean. So delirious by the end, he believed ghosts were riding with him. "During immeasurable periods," he later wrote, "I seemed to extend outside my plane and body. . . . It was an experience in which both the intellectual and sensate were replaced by . . . a matterless awareness."

We drive on, into Kingman for a late dinner, before turning north for Las Vegas. After eating, I realize that I've left my wallet in the restaurant and jog back inside. When I return to the parking lot again, next to the Skylark, a man and a woman are getting out of a van with a handpainted, black-lettered sign hung on the hull that reads *From Auschwitz to Arizona, Boston to Bosnia, Psychiatry Kills*. The man wears a leather pouch slung over his shoulder and the woman has gray hair that falls to the middle of her back, though she looks quite young. Because they are walking right toward me, our gazes lock a second too long, and then suddenly, inescapably, I feel obligated to say something.

"Hey, what's with the sign?" They both look back at the van, then at me again. The man smiles. "The male unit is more susceptible to mind control," he tells me. I make a show of pondering.

"But why does psychiatry kill more than, say, dentistry?" I ask.

"Dentistry is tool-based," says the woman. As if that's enough.

"Right," I say, shuffling toward the Skylark. Exhaust pours from the tailpipe and Harvey sits in silhouette. The whole car is suddenly throbbing to a classic rock station, the baseline from Heart's "Magic Man." I surmise that buttons have been pushed, dials experimented with, and whether Harvey's just given up or is truly partial to the song, I don't know. But his head appears in the side window, his sil-

ver hair glowing in a pool of sodium light, his eagle nose proud and
true, as the words enwrap him:

Try to understand
Try to understand
Try, try, try to understand . . . He's a magic man.
He's got the magic hands, Momma. . . .

The couple from the van glance between him and me, perplexed.
"My grandfather," I lie. And because the conversation is already of a
certain tenor, and because I don't really care anymore, I decide to tell
them the truth. "He's the guy who did the autopsy on Albert
Einstein," I say. "We've got part of Einstein's brain in the trunk. We're
going to give it back to his granddaughter."

They don't question it, don't even blink, but they're not pleased,
either. People controlling other people's brains. This is the very stuff
of their nightmares. "Seems incongruous," says the male unit. "Like
dialing a disconnected telephone number. No, I don't agree. We're
carpet-cleaners and Scientologists." He hands me a business card. On
it there's a name and a company—Magic Carpet Cleaning.

"I'd be glad to talk to you more about this whenever you feel like
it," he tells me. "Call anytime. But, right now, if you'd excuse us,
we're starving." And they disappear into the restaurant. I open the car
door, and fall into 1976, circa *Dreamboat Annie.*

"YOU LIKE THIS TUNE?" I yell over the music, just because I feel
like yelling a little, then turn it down.

"Way-ell, heh-heh . . . we had a little problem there," says Harvey,
fiddling his fingers. Twenty-four hours ago, I might have indulged
him: gently asked him what happened, laughed with him about it
to make him feel better, found a suitable station for him. But I don't
now. I start the car, swoop from our parking space and floor it up
Route 93, a two-lane shot, at eighty miles an hour. I'm so tired
that the approaching headlights all come in fours instead of twos;

besieged by traffic, I squint with one eye closed, just to let it rest. Days become minutes and minutes become days. Approaching the Hoover Dam—lit like a small alpine city in a ravine, powerlines strung like uranium stanzas in the air—I stupidly pass a VW Bug and by the hairbreadth grace of God just barely avoid a head-on collision with a lumbering truck. Its lights, broken out like jewels on the grill, spell "Marianne," the name of my mother.

Las Vegas. We arrive from above, and below the city appears like a coronation of shimmering brightness, like so much shattered glass thrown by the fistful over a sandy floor, a high-desert Hong Kong of possibility. "Sunday midnight is our busiest time of the week," says the woman who checks us in to the Excalibur Hotel and Casino. "There's no freaking explaining it."

Sunday? It sounds like some long-lost point of reference. It didn't even occur to me that it was Sunday. And now we stand amid the ballyhooing hordes: pale-skinned easterners and leather-skinned westerners, bikers and accountants, cowboy-hatted and Indian-vested, big-haired and bald as cue balls, imperial on free drinks and soaring on the oxygen-enriched air pumping into this church of big dreams, everyone taking their stab at Instamatic riches.

Harvey seems overwhelmed, his Quaker sensibilities so jangled that he humps straight up to one of our cheesy eighteenth-floor rooms, which are tricked out like a cardboard castle set for a high-school production of *Camelot*. He again refuses help with his luggage, has the brain slung over his shoulder in the duffel and tosses it in the closet. Out the window the Strip is molten and alive. But he closes the shade.

"Good night, Senator," I say, and he looks at me as if he's in the presence of someone unraveling, which he may be.

Suddenly wide awake, I go back downstairs and roam. One man at a five-dollar blackjack table, a short, tightly bundled guy who smells of lime aftershave, is abstractedly addressing the male dealer in gambler clichés and porn-movie dialogue. "Oh yeah, baby! . . . Yeah, baby! . . . Give it to me! . . . Hit me! . . . Oh yeah! . . . Hold right there! . . . Feels good!"

Soon, he is sitting alone. As are others like him. These are men so sunk down inside themselves that they don't give a prostitute working the place a second look when she cozies up to them. Personally, I'm feeling pretty good, accept as many watered-down gin-and-tonics as get offered to me by the cocktail waitresses (four), lose some quick money at the roulette table (sixty dollars), and then, feeling a little less good, regroup in the Minstrel's Lounge with more liquid refreshment. The bar opens out to the casino, so I sit and watch the various dramas unfold. And what strikes me is how lonely everyone seems, how the bleating and beeping of slot machines or the robotic silence of the dealers—how the free drinks and cheap prime rib dinners and the surface camaraderie of everybody—are all part and parcel of a kingdom that could care less about its subjects.

If people come here to escape their lives, I find the Vegas spectacle throws me back on mine. When I called Sara back last night, I woke her, but then we talked for a good hour. About nothing and everything. Like we always have. A reminder that, somewhere back there in the past—and perhaps in the future—I still exist. Almost finished with her book, Sara was plotting what she was going to do the second she broke loose from her computer—ski trips and movies to see and sushi to eat. She sounded ebullient, her voice a river current, the kind that makes you see colors. We talked about the possibility of rendezvousing in San Francisco after Harvey and I have finished our little mission. Thinking of it now, in the Minstrel's Lounge, makes me feel good for a moment, and then, after I've peaked on that bonhomie, suddenly, dismally alone.

There's an older couple sitting next to me, minding their own business, chatting quietly to each other. After my earlier repartee with the Scientologist carpet-cleaners in the restaurant parking lot, I try to think before speaking this time. When put to it, I can be an all right conversationalist. But I find openings are always tricky. Something like, How are you folks this evening? is such a dead end and I can't say it without feeling as if I sound like a bad Western movie cliché. I consider the obvious—Winning any?—but then it's such a loser's question. And before I know it, my mouth is moving, again.

"I'm on a trip," I say, "and I was wondering what you two know about Albert Einstein?"

The husband's eyebrows shoot up and he gives his wife a look like: *Flee.* "I don't know anything about him, really," he says in a Yankee accent, "and I don't care one way or the other. I'm just trying to have fun."

"I don't know anything either," chimes his wife cheerfully. "Just that he was a genius or something."

"I'm traveling with the doctor who owns Einstein's brain," I say, "and we're going to California to give it to Einstein's granddaughter." The man folds his arms and looks at me straight on. "Whatever makes you happy," he says. Then he digs into his pocket, plops a bill on the bar, and shielding his wife from me, gets away.

Lonely as I am, it's weirdly empowering, this sudden ability to repel people by innocently invoking Einstein's name. So I go wandering. At an empty blackjack table, I ask a dealer, a Korean guy with a mustache, about Einstein. "I don't know anything about him," he says, "but that man over there should be able to help you." He points to his manager, a white guy with a mustache. He barely lets me finish before responding, "Haven't seen him in here tonight. Sorry, pal."

I try again, with the friendliest-looking man I can find. He's middle-aged and round-bellied, like his group of friends, all wearing University of Wisconsin sweatshirts emblazoned with the school's mascot, Bucky Badger. They're nothing but laughter and smiles until I smile back and ask what they know about Albert Einstein. Bucky Badger furrows his brow. "Why do you want to know?" he demands.

"Has anyone ever told you about E=mc²? Has anyone in this casino bothered to tell you that?"

I explained that, no, no one has, and that I am driving Einstein's brain cross-country. At the mention of the brain, he doesn't miss a beat, becomes impatient. "Let's bury the damn brain and be done with it," he says, as if he's been in on the debate since the beginning.

I try one last time, a cocktail waitress with a beehive of blond hair. She stands in a short black and gold dress, looking like someone's risqué aunt in age denial at a wedding. Still, she has fabulous legs. When I ask her if she happens to know what Albert Einstein is famous for, her jaw drops.

"You're kidding," she says. "You must be kidding me. Is there a hidden camera around here? You're the fifth guy to ask me that tonight. . . ." Her voice is pinched with anger. "You know what? I do know who he is. . . ." We've known each other less than twenty seconds, and yet it feels as if we've lived a lifetime of emotions. "He invented the atom bomb, and I happen to think he's terrible."

"See, I'm a reader," she says, balling her fists. "If you want to find me, come look in the library because I'm studying to be an attorney. An attorney of law." I assure her that I mean no offense by the question, only I've been asking everyone because I'm so tired I can't sleep and because I've been driving cross-country with Einstein's brain in the trunk of a rental car.

"And who are you?" she asks. "Who the hell are you? Why don't you show me some ID before I have you kicked out of here." But even as I reflexively go to show her my license, she's waving security over. There's a commotion, a burly casino employee in a short-sleeved shirt with biceps the size of a Big Mac asks if I'm here to gamble or just to harass the help. I tell him that it's not what it seems, but then I'm not at all sure what it seems. He cuts me off, mercifully. "It's time for beddy-bye, fella," he says, and I don't disagree. Just head up to my chamber in the castle tower and then pass out, matterlessly unaware.

The morning brings sun and sandpapery air. A new feeling and freshness. A proverbial spring in the step. Forgiveness. Well-rested, Harvey and I go for breakfast, but huge lines trail out of the Roundtable Buffet and Sherwood Forest Café. So we watch a juggler dressed in green tights work the crowd—"Oh boy, whatta juggler!" says Harvey. Later, we gather our bags and head through the casino for the castle door, Harvey with the brain slung over his shoulder again. We pause at a bank of slot machines. A group of grandmothers from Iowa give Harvey a quick once-over, then go back to their spinning lemons and limes and sevens.

I pull a couple of coins from my pocket as a peace offering. "For good luck," I tell him. Until now, Harvey hasn't been keen on gambling, but for my sake he slides a quarter in the slot machine and reluctantly pulls the lever. In a way, this moment stands against everything he believes, for in Harvey's world, life has never been a game of chance. And anyway, he already has his jackpot, slung over his shoulder.

But then there's a moment as the fruit spins, as the possibility of a jackpot revolves before him, when Harvey's face lights briefly at the prospect of what could be, of what one little stroke of luck might bring. Sometimes even the believers forget what they believe.

Part Four

17 ◆ Here and Gone, Forever

We make Los Angeles at rush hour. After three days of driving through the desert, the city explodes in a psychedelic flash of lush palm trees and red taillights on I-10. We pass a gold-earringed Asian woman, driving a red BMW with a vanity plate that reads 2SUCCESS. It seems the cars here—the Hummers, Jags, and Benzes; the Accords, Jettas, even the Escorts—gleam with their own declaration of erotic or financial prowess: 8MILL; ORGAZ; MONEY. As if everyone is trying to leave some indelible impression of themselves in this five-second casting call of heavy traffic.

On the radio, we get an action-news update about a disgruntled circus clown who's stolen a car, busting for freedom on the interstate headed north, and then an American psycho who's just been caught at Steven Spielberg's house with a bag containing handcuffs, duct tape, and a razor knife. The day's dubious leading men. Packed in, moving five abreast, we somehow cloverleaf onto the 405, headed north, and end up lost for the first time all trip. When we finally escape the highway, we exit in the wrong direction, driving inland through Beverly Hills to West Hollywood, though we're looking for what's directly behind us: Santa Monica and the sea.

Los Angeles has always baffled my New England sensibilities. Not only do I not understand a place with only one real season to speak of—sunshine—I'm disoriented by the fact that a building from the 1950s seems ancient around here. And that even bus drivers look tan and spectacular. And that when you eat out, people watch the front door to see who's arrived as if they're watching television.

West Hollywood oscillates between trendy and seedy, depending on the block and the clientele on the sidewalk. There are boutiques and bodegas, comic book stores and fancy eateries. At a gas station, I approach a stocky, balding guy in short sleeves and a tie. He enthusiastically offers directions and then asks where I'm from. I obligingly spill everything, without a trace of guilt. And once he absorbs it, he looks as if I just plucked a hair from his head, stands there wide-eyed and stunned. "No fuck, you got Einstein's brain right over there?" he says, blinking. "No fucking way! Right in that trunk? The car with the little old man? Are you making a fucking movie of this? Holy fuck!" He pulls out a business card with a picture of himself on it, sporting a full head of half-synthetic hair. He's a field engineer for Kodak. "That was in my Hair Club days," he says, without hesitation. "Einstein's fucking brain! What the fuck is next? Aliens, right?"

About five blocks down, we realize that Hair Club has given us bum directions. We drift to the curb and ask for help from the first person who appears on the other side of our rolled-down window: a cross-dresser in body-hugging black leather with thin, shaved legs that seem six feet long and a tiara of some sort in his hair. He's an attractive woman and knows it, bends into the window seductively, and gives precise directions, then says. "Hurry now, y'all don't want to miss that romantic sunset over the Pacific." After a half block, Harvey glances once over his shoulder. "Way-ell, we sure asked the right person," he says.

We drive the brain down Sunset and Wilshire, past new office buildings and the empty Ambassador Hotel, a hulking, black-windowed coffin where Bobby Kennedy was assassinated, then down Rodeo and Hollywood, past fancy shops and fancy people, and it's all déjà vu. The brain has been here before, three times in fact, when it still resided in Einstein's head. Describing one of Einstein's visits to

Los Angeles, the humorist Will Rogers said, "He came here for rest and seclusion. He ate with everybody, talked with everybody, posed for everybody . . . attended every luncheon, every dinner, every movie opening, every marriage, and two-thirds of the divorces. In fact, he made himself such a good fellow that nobody had the nerve to ask what his theory was."

And certainly, among the palm trees and sunshine, among the glitter and yawn of Hollywood, the Einsteins were curious animals. Dressed like a provincial watchmaker and his wife, the couple came, speaking in thick German accents. Einstein's forgetfulness was endearing, if already somewhat legendary. And Elsa herself was a short-sighted, earthy woman who, mistaking a flower arrangement for a salad, once served herself an orchid. Not surprisingly, Charlie Chaplin took a shine to Einstein and invited him and Elsa to the world premiere of his film *City Lights*.

But the FBI was not amused by the friendship. Acting on a tip received by J. Edgar Hoover from a former RKO Studios executive, agents undertook an exhaustive investigation, trying to verify a mysterious encounter at the Ambassador Hotel that allegedly had taken place between the executive—whom I'll call Harmon, as his name has been expunged from the FBI record—and Einstein, who Harmon claimed was introduced to him as "the brain that was setting up Hollywood . . . for the big Communist push." Harmon, the RKO executive, was brought to Einstein by a supposed operative—a Bolshevik who ran a photography studio in the hotel lobby as a front, and who led Harmon to a suite upstairs where Harmon claimed he saw both Einstein and Chaplin huddled in a meeting. According to FBI report LA 105-1636, the Bolshevik allegedly told Harmon that "Einstein was organizing all the big studio figures, stars, and all the leading directors and writers.

"We've got them in our hand and the Doctor has never failed on one," he said, "give him an hour and he convinces you." Harmon resisted, blasting them all as "crackpots." But then later he lost his job, implying that he had become a Hollywood casualty because of the anti-Communist stand he took that day. His allegations, however, were never proven.

At dusk, Harvey and I finally reach Santa Monica swaddled in a warm ocean wind. The point, the goal, the grail of today, has been to see the ocean, to see a billion gallons of steel-blue water from Japan crashing these gold beaches, container ships bobbing on the horizon. And when we come down to the beach and the sea stretches endlessly before us, I retrieve that memory of the Atlantic as I saw it eight days ago—green and whipped-up in a high wind—around a bend on the train to Connecticut. Which brings back my parents and my grandfather and the miles we've driven, and suddenly my eyes well up with inexplicable tears because I've finally let down, and Harvey, he cracks the window and puts his hand out into the air, lets it swoop down and dive in the currents, just to feel California.

There's an amazing release that comes when you drive coast to coast, when you plug one ocean into another in your mind. And the wake of your travels fills with a kind of awe and love for everyone and everything and every animal and every roadside diner you've seen between the two. Which is why I'm completely unprepared for what comes next.

He's the Pakistani check-in man at a Days Inn on Santa Monica Boulevard where we stop for the night. He sports the generic solid-striped, red and blue tie of every night-man who's checked us into a hotel on this trip, wears a name tag: Joseph. He has a thick, bristly push broom of a mustache. And his mouth is already moving before I realize he's talking to me. "Hello, my friend, hello. Did you see the network premiere of *Schindler's List* last night on TV? You know, the Steven Spielberg film?"

Fishing a credit card from my wallet—Harvey waiting with the brain in the car—I rise from my stupor. "Excuse me?"

"Yes, my friend, *Schindler's List*. I see your nose and I think: Jew. A fine, large Jewish nose. But if you had lived with the Nazis, well, my friend, you would be dead now."

This is a confusing hypothetical. I don't doubt its veracity, yet I can't figure how we've gotten from my simply wanting two rooms for the night to the size of my nose, which, albeit a degree larger than normal, isn't much bigger than Joseph's, to a sudden scenario in which I'm Jewish and the Nazis want me dead. To show that I regard what he's saying—for he could be dangerous—I agree, though I admit that the nose belongs to a sorely lapsed Catholic.

"I'm Christian, too," he says, "but the Jew is God's chosen in the Old Testament. I am a Christian, but Jesus was a Jew. Moses was a Jew. Abraham was a Jew. David was a Jew. Elijah was a Jew. . . ."

The list goes on and on. It's mesmerizing, and when I get the feeling he's just getting warmed up I think about trying to insert a name, just to derail him long enough to get the two rooms. The only one that comes to mind is Einstein, of course, which I automatically blurt out. Joseph quickly says, "That guy's a Jew, too."

"I know," I say. "You're naming Jewish people, right?"

"Prophets," says Joseph. "Jewish *prophets*."

"Oh," I say. Then again without thinking: "And Einstein's not?"

Joseph looks puzzled, and so I try to clarify. "I mean, some people in this world think of him as a god." At that Joseph's face drops. "Oh no, you are crazy," he says. "Ha, ha, ha!" He pretends to clear wax from the canal of his right ear, though he seems to be trembling. "Who? Einstein was a god? You ask that kind of question. You are very stupid. Einstein invented more than a hundred things, yes, but you ask that kind of question to me? People are sick. A lot of crazy people. You would be in big trouble if Einstein was a god. How can you ask me such a stupid question?"

The phone rings, and a complex transformation takes place on his face—the unknitting of his brow, a smile working up under the heavy bench press of a frown—until his hand is on the receiver. Until he's suddenly all light and feathers, fresh cream and strawberries. Then he answers in a singsong "Hell-ooo, Days Inn." He chews a fingernail. "Right, right, yes, Wednesday? We have room . . . ninety-eight dollars. Yes, fine. Smoking or nonsmoking, my friend? . . . Oh, that's fine. We'll look forward to seeing you. Have a wonderful evening." He doesn't seem to write anything down, and when he hangs up, he locks right back on me—goes from mild-mannered Bill Bixby to the Incredible Hulk again—and begins listing the things that he believes Einstein invented.

"Relativity, number one," says Joseph, counting with his fingers for me. "And then he invented, for example, zero. You can't make ten without zero. You can't make a hundred or a thousand, either. You understand. You got it now?"

"Yes," I say, then I ask him if he has a couple of rooms. But he's having none of it. "You say Einstein is a god," says Joseph. "No, Jesus is a god. Einstein is dead, no? Jesus came back three days later, you understand, my friend? Einstein is a filthy man, you know, someone who had pets. You need to study Albert Einstein. Study first. Okay? . . . What can I say to you? Who say Einstein is a god?"

"There are people who think very highly of him," I say.

Joseph's mustache twitches, and then he bursts forth, "I am shocked myself! It's terrible what you say! He's a man, man! He's a sidekick! He's not God. He cannot give life. Jesus give life!" At this he reaches over the counter and puts his hand a few inches from my mouth, growling, "If I close your mouth and nose, you will die. Einstein cannot give . . . Jesus give life, you understand?"

The phone rings again, and Joseph takes a step back, regathers himself, then turns on the soft-serve. "Days Inn, may I kindly help you . . . for tonight? . . . tomorrow? We are sold out . . . yes, yes, Thursday we have rooms. How many people? Yes, three rooms . . . that's two seventy-four plus tax. . . . Fine, then. Yes, very good, my friend. We'll look forward to your arrival." No sooner than the phone lands in its cradle, Joseph explodes. "Einstein a god? Ha, ha, ha! I cannot sleep a couple nights now. Stop insulting me! Jesus is a god! Einstein cannot save anybody's life!" Then he repeats his half lunge at me and says, "If for three minutes, your nose and mouth closeth you will be dead right here and Einstein will not do a thing about it!"

I must admit that the man scares me. I take a step back. "You know, I was still actually wondering if you had a couple of rooms?" I say. And suddenly, I'm no longer Jewish or a heretic or someone that the desk man feels compelled to strangle. Grudgingly, Joseph coughs up two keys, takes an imprint of my Visa card, and then I go out to retrieve Harvey, whom I then hustle back through the lobby, where Joseph is thankfully busy with newly arrived customers. If he's Pakistan, then I've suddenly become India, and this hotel lobby is Kashmir. A lesson in how easy war is. A big nose, a couple of offhanded queries, and then—kaboom!—a little jihad. Just as I shut the door to my room upstairs and double-lock it, the phone rings. Joseph. "Now you come back downstairs this instant," he says. "I have much to show you. I can't believe my ears. Einstein a god. Ha, ha, ha. You are a very stupid person."

※

When we decided on taking the southern route, the idea suited Harvey fine, in part because he wanted to visit a Los Angeles doctor to whom he once sent slices of Einstein's brain for research. Now that we're here, however, he says he can't seem to reach him. And then, when I ask who it is, he can't recall his name, either. Meanwhile, I've made plans to meet Roger Richman, the president of his own celebrity-licensing agency and the man who represents the beneficiaries of the estate of Albert Einstein, Hebrew University in Jerusalem. It is Richman who helps to keep Einstein's legacy alive in our consumer culture. He polices trademark infringements, hawks trade shows for Einstein contraband, and decides just how the image of the physicist will be used in advertisements and on merchandise around the world. When I first called Richman from Kansas and told him that

I was heading his way with Harvey and Einstein's brain, he was curt. "The brain is at the Smithsonian," he said. "And I'd rather not have you bring that man along." And although the brain has never been near the Smithsonian—and is authentically still in our trunk—I'm forced to make up some polite excuse when I leave Harvey, something about seeing a friend. I drop him at the beach, where he finds a senior center and spends the day writing postcards, making pals, playing cards. Then I guiltily head over to Richman's Beverly Hills office.

Richman, fifty-three, is a big, powerful man with big, powerful ideas and a full head of thickly parted, natural hair. He wears an Izod-type green short-sleeved shirt. He greets me by saying, "You got the brain with you?" And then he starts laughing, a contagious, raucous laugh that puts me at ease. He ushers me into his office, a large, cluttered room strewn with prized possessions, as well as unlicensed celebrity products. On the walls are hung all sorts of genuine celebrity bric-a-brac: Jimmy Durante's coonskin cap, a framed letter written by Marlene Dietrich ("That's priceless," says Richman, "if I put that up for auction, I'd get twenty-five thousand dollars"), and a check signed by Clark Gable. He also owns a cool pair of Steve McQueen's boots. Before we begin to chat, he places a tape recorder on the desk and, in this most self-referential of cities, announces that he is taping for the autobiography he intends to write someday. "I would like to say that I'm a marketing genius," he says.

Richman proceeds to tell me the illustrious history of Richman. How, eighteen years ago, the son of Bela Lugosi sued Universal Studios for a percentage of profits made from the image of his father as Dracula. And although he lost the lawsuit, the judgment contained one paragraph stating that whereas the studio owned the rights to Dracula and the family did not have a right to control Lugosi's image, no one else had the right to appropriate it, either. With that one paragraph, Richman set off for swap meets, stalking the stalls, picking up all kinds of items that illegally appropriated the images of dead stars. Then he went after the infringers on behalf of the families.

In 1983, he drove to Sacramento with the sons of John Wayne and Harpo Marx and the grandson of W. C. Fields, and together they argued for a celebrity rights act, which legally assured that no one may use the name, voice, or picture of a deceased personality without permission from the family. Then the group made the same argument in New York State, where they were called "a group of tribal headhunters" by a lawyer representing Time Inc. "It was the proudest moment of my life," Richman says.

What he's become in these past two decades is the Upholder of Dead Celebrity, the Protector of the Afterimage. Among the estates he has recently serviced are those of Louis Armstrong, Sigmund Freud, Mae West, and the Wright brothers, as well as a personal favorite of mine, none other than Sherlock Holmes himself, Basil Rathbone. Until he lost a recent bidding war, he had Marilyn Monroe and remembers the day someone came to him with a Marilyn doll. "I said, 'That doesn't look like Marilyn Monroe. And if it doesn't look like Marilyn Monroe, it's not going to sell.' So I had a little sculpture studio and my little house in Hollywood and . . . I brought out some tools and I straightened out her cheeks, and I did, you know, certain things to fix it up. It sold very well. Subsequent dolls, that I didn't have anything to do with and weren't an accurate rendition, failed."

Sitting there, learning from Richman, it occurs to me that some people wake up in the morning and sell bagels, some fight fires, and some sculpt Marilyn dolls, reveling in the glamour of dead people, in the memories and photographs of another era. In the same way that Harvey has lived in the glow of Einstein's brain, Richman lives in the glow of Einstein, the ghost—his biggest client. He claims he employs five law firms domestically and as many abroad to protect his client, paying up to forty thousand dollars a month for their services. He shows me a stack of papers, dictionary thick. "All of these are Albert Einstein infringements," he declares proudly. He shows me a famous photograph of Einstein sticking his tongue out. "We never allow this picture to be used," he says fussily. "You know people come back to me and say, 'Who are you to say we can't use this when he stuck his tongue out and he knew photographers were there?' and I say, 'Hey, I'm running a public trust; it's incumbent upon me to protect these people.' "

Richman won't reveal how much money he and Hebrew University make annually from Einstein, but he admits it's more than from any other client, totalling somewhere in the seven figures. I remind him that Einstein never allowed his name or image to serve as a product endorsement during his life. "Money only appeals to selfishness and irresistibly invites abuse," the physicist said. "Can anyone imagine Moses, Jesus, or Gandhi with the moneybags of Carnegie?" So wouldn't he object to himself selling Nikon cameras or Pepsi-Cola now? Richman dismissively waves his hand, assuring me that all the profits go to scholarships at Hebrew University.

Then, to show me just how bleak a world without Roger Richman can be, he leads me to a large cardboard box across the room. It's full of black-market desecrations—"horrible, horrible stuff," Richman says, wincing. A greeting card with Mae West urinating through an hourglass, one of Marilyn Monroe snorting cocaine. There's John Wayne toilet paper ("It's rough!—It's tough! And it doesn't take crap off anyone!"), a vial of Elvis's sweat ("Now you can let his perspiration be an inspiration"), and a box of cotton balls emblazoned with the words "Brando's Balls." But the pièce de résistance, the succès de scandale, is wrapped in paper with rubber bands around it. "I always keep him in his house," says Richman. "I never take him out."

Richman places it in my hands, and I unwrap it slowly to find eight inches of hard rubber topped by the smiley-faced head of Ronald Reagan. It was this very dildo that Richman waved on the floor of the California statehouse to make his point—"I HAVE HERE IN MY HANDS A SEXUAL DEVICE!" he bellowed to the shocked assemblage—and that pleases him.

Once the Gipper has been wrapped and replaced in the box, we tour the rest of the office. I'm shown W. C. Fields's hundred-proof gin and vodka and Dr. Freud's Pillow Talk, a bootleg pillow that speaks when you pull a string. "Vi don't you lay down on zee couch. . . . Hmmmm, ha, I see, relax, let your conscious . . . aha . . ."

In order to put his own client list in perspective, Richman recently called the Screen Actors Guild and found that about eighteen thousand actors have died in this century. "How many are marketable today?" asks Richman, throwing his arms open in disbelief. "Twenty! These are the most talented people that ever lived . . . but most people are here and gone forever. You know, you have your fifteen minutes of fame and that's it."

So then why does fame matter at all? I ask. And why are we so obsessed with it? He begins by quoting Thoreau: " 'The mass of men lead lives of quiet desperation.'

"They'll never be an Elizabeth Taylor," he says. "Their hopes are their dreams and their dreams are on TV and their dreams are of watching these beautiful chests walking into the Academy Awards in gorgeous gowns and they live for that. That's why communism failed. It never gave people any hope. That's why democracy has been so successful. The American dream, it's based on hope. . . . As long as you have money, you go right to the top."

He continues. "When I travel into the heartland of America—I go backpacking a lot—and talk about what I'm doing, oh, these people, they won't let me shut up. They just ask question after question after question. I'm like a hero to them. Around here, no one cares. Dead stars, oh, forget it. You're an agent for the dead, you're a joke, c'mon."

But Richman tells me that he's having the last laugh, in no small part thanks to Einstein, who's gone global. In Japan, Einstein's image is used in a commercial for a video game called 3DO; in Hungary, his mug is plastered on billboards for a local telephone company; in South Africa, he advertises insurance. "He's the most widely recognized human being that ever lived," declares Richman. "In China"—

where he has recently brokered a deal for Einstein T-shirts—"they're limited to one child per family, and every single parent calls their one child 'my little Einstein.' " He smiles at the thought.

"China is a cultural wasteland," he says emphatically, standing in his own museum of cowboy boots and dildos. "They've never heard of John Wayne. They've never heard of Steve McQueen. They've never seen any of their movies. But Einstein, they know."

18 ◆ Bat Wings and Superstring

When I think about all of the possible fates for Einstein's brain—being cloned or shot into space; being auctioned for millions or rebuilt and taken on tour; being stolen by a madman or terrorists—I think mostly about a story, an auguring of sorts, that Harvey tells me when we leave Los Angeles that night for San Jose, a five-hour drive up through the San Joaquin Valley. As I've finally hit the wall, exhausted and strung-out, Harvey is absolutely chipper and chatty.

It happened on vacation nearly thirty years ago, on the Outer Banks of North Carolina. Harvey remembers the beach on a bright day, the ocean glittering, a nearly Algerian sun. He remembers combing for shells with his granddaughters, and in the distance spotting a glassy gray-blue thing, like a body. Nobody knew what it was. And just like that, the girls raced toward it, then around it, chanting, "Grandpa, Grandpa!"

"Way-ell, what do we have here?" Harvey wondered aloud, mind whirring with calculations: newly dead. Two or three hundred pounds. Diseased? Drowned in a net? No trace of one, though. An incredible specimen. Harvey remembers staring at it, at the sheen of its Polyprene skin. At its fluked tail. The whole spectacular muscle of it. The light turning it emerald. *Tursiops truncatus.* Who knew dolphins had eyelids?

And then Harvey did what came most naturally: He drew a jackknife and plunged the blade into the dolphin's underbelly, flensing the skin. I wonder about this, seeing your grandfather suddenly knifing a dead dolphin. I mean, did the girls scream, or immediately come close to see its heart and the few sardines in its stomach? Either way, Harvey performed an autopsy right there on the beach. And then he stuck the knife in the dolphin's skull and ruched back a cowl of flesh to reveal the brain, which he deftly cut loose. He remembers that: the brain in his hands. The brain. In his hands again. The girls dancing. "Eeeeeewwwwww!"

"The convolutions were amazing," he says to me now as we pass glorious sights, fields of avocados and limes, in the dark. "More than a human brain. More ridges and convolutions than our brains." He remembers fixing it in a formaldehyde solution, and later, at the vacation's end, taking it home with him. As he speaks, I find that my mind has somehow replaced the dolphin's brain with Einstein's. He says he kept it for many years, occasionally inspecting it. He treasured it as both a memory and a specimen. When I ask what happened to it, he can't remember. Just remembers the story.

"What the deuces became of that?" he says, racking his own brain now. "I really wonder where I put that darn thing."

⚛

It didn't occur to me that San Jose would be a must-see stop for Harvey, but then he's sprung a little surprise on me: He's giving a talk on Einstein's brain in San Jose tomorrow. He apparently called a woman named Sarah Gonzalez, who had written to him a few years ago randomly asking for a piece of the brain. When she heard from Harvey, she felt that the Lord God had intervened on her behalf. Ever since his call, she has been busy informing San Jose of our arrival, contacting the mayor and the local media, trying to set up a dinner party for the leading lights in her community, and arranging for Harvey and Einstein's brain to visit with students at Independence High School, one of the biggest in the country. But of course this is the first I've heard about it.

Gonzalez has reserved us rooms at the Biltmore Hotel, but when we arrive, around two A.M., out on some industrial edge of San Jose, there is only one available room left, with a sole double bed. "Why, I'm sure it's a big one," says Harvey with a nervous chuckle. I ask for a cot. And by the time I roll it into the room, the duffeled brain is up on the television with the weather on and Harvey is snorkeling through his suitcase, each item of his clothing—his silk pajamas, a 49ers sweatshirt, his slippers, and a dress shirt—wrapped in cellophane. He has brought two suits for tomorrow, neatly folded like big bat wings in his case, a black winter worsted wool and a baby-blue leisure-type suit.

Without ceremony, I collapse on the cot, and no sooner do I hit the pillow than I'm wide awake, the road running through my head in white dotted lines. And then I keep thinking about Harvey's suitcase. It's as if I've seen inside the body of a living man only to find all the organs cellophaned. I keep my head buried as Harvey putters around the room. When he spoke to Gonzalez a few days ago to confirm plans, he promised to call when we arrived, though she probably assumed he wouldn't ring her at two-thirty A.M. Nonetheless, the White Rabbit picks up the phone, dials her number, and wakes her to let her know we're here, then hangs up.

I can hear him running water in the sink, clearing his throat, ironing. I can hear him ferreting through his crinkly clothes, then perusing his various articles—mimeographed pages taken from old articles on Einstein, ones that, I'll later discover, outline a general, layperson's biography of the scientist—preparing for his lecture. And then I hear something that sounds like an electric toothbrush. Before the sun rises, he finally goes to bed. His breathing slows and then grows deeper like a river running into pools. Instead of snoring, there's a sweet lowing in his gasps for air, and finally it puts me to sleep, too.

When I wake at eight the next morning, Harvey's crunching loudly on caramel corn. He's half dressed, having opted for the black suit with black suspenders and a gray turtleneck, though the weather is verging on summer. Sarah Gonzalez calls and announces that she's in the lobby, nearly an hour early. My head is pounding, but while Harvey primps, I go to meet her. She's the only person at the bar, busily doing something with her hands. When I come closer, I realize that she is pressing on a set of acrylic fingernails. For a moment, she doesn't notice that I'm standing there, and we both admire her handiwork. When she looks up, she seems surprised. "Oh," she says, extends an automatic hand with half new nails and half bitten ones, and peeks around me for Harvey and the brain.

Sarah Gonzalez is a short, pretty, quick-moving Filipino woman with black-and-gold sunglasses and an ostentatious emerald car. In her mood and mannerisms she reminds me of a brushfire in a high wind. She personifies the immigrant's dream. A former executive secretary, she is now the president of her own company, Pacific Connections, which markets biomass energy conversion—or, as she puts it, "turning cornstalks to megawatts." Next week, she tells me, she will be in Manila meeting with the Filipino president in hopes of bringing the gift of energy—more lights and televisions—to her country of birth.

When Harvey comes chugging out, she pales, then starts forward. "Dr. Harvey, I presume," says Gonzalez, clucking and bowing her head. "I can't believe there is someone living and breathing who was so close to Einstein." But what's this? Harvey's removed the brain from the gray duffel and now holds the Tupperware container in his hand, though the plastic is clouded enough that you can really only see the urine-colored liquid inside. It's my first indirect glimpse of the brain all trip, and suddenly, it's as if we're not fully clothed. Even as Harvey palms the Tupperware container in the lobby, I feel a need to hide it. Gonzalez herself doesn't notice, treats Harvey with the respect and solemnity usually granted an archbishop, rushes us into her Mercury Grand Marquis. She's a woman who enjoys the liberal use of first names. "Mike, what do you think of this scandal, Mike?"

she asks. "This—how do you say?—campaign-contribution scandal, Mike?" She is perhaps the most persistently friendly person I've ever met.

Harvey sits in the front bucket seat, sunk down in the fine Italian leather, the fabric of his own suit dull and aged by comparison; there's a tiny hole in one knee of his heavy suit pants. He clears his throat repeatedly and starts to chuckle. "Do you know a fella named Burroughs, William Burroughs?" She's never heard of him. Harvey tries again.

"Where does Gates live?"

"Bill Gates, Dr. Harvey? That would be Seattle, I think. Isn't that right, Mike? Seattle, Mike?"

"I thought that fella lived right here in Silicon Valley," says Harvey, hawkeyeing the streets suspiciously. A little later on, Harvey's more at ease, sets himself chuckling again. "Those are the funniest-looking trees," he says.

"They are palm trees, Dr. Harvey," says Gonzalez.

We're given a brief tour of "old San Jose"—a collection of Day-Glo houses that look brand-new—then stop at Gonzalez's house, a comfortable though tightly packed bungalow on a cul-de-sac where she lives with her husband and five children, some in high school, some in college. A full drum kit is set up in the living room. One gets the impression that when this house is full there's probably nothing here but love and a hell of a racket. Meeting her husband, I retract her title and claim *him* as the friendliest person I've ever met. "Oh, Dr. Harvey, what does it feel like to be you?" he asks. He serves us cookies and milk. His neighbor—a slightly skittish Vietnam vet whom the Gonzalezes call the "glue of the neighborhood"—stops by to borrow a stick of butter for a pineapple upside-down cake he's baking and suddenly he, too, is in the living room, eating cookies and milk on a sunny Wednesday morning, nodding seriously as Sarah Gonzalez springs the whole Harvey saga on him. Somehow, he doesn't seem to understand, has missed the part about Einstein's brain, and then just looks as if he's in utter pain. At the first distraction, he vanishes out the front door.

"Oh," says Sarah Gonzalez when she turns around to find him gone with the gentle slam of the screen door.

We gather ourselves for the ride over to Independence High. After photographs have been taken on the front lawn, we go to leave. Harvey sniffs the air, lets a soft wind cover him with the scent of magnolia, and seems to disappear into the past for a moment. He reaches down and lifts a pinecone from the perfect, chemical-fed turf, holds it up, admiring its symmetry, and, for reasons of his own, pockets it.

At Independence High, a golf cart and a student driver pick us up at the front entrance and whisk us a half mile through campus to a special teacher lunch for Harvey. There are cut-up subs from a local sandwich shop, cans of soda, piles of napkins, and big bags of potato chips. At its humming climax, there are about twenty-five people in the room, teachers and a few invited students, handpicked for exhibiting their own traces of brilliance in science class, in hopes that their close proximity to the brain may imbue them with some of the Einstein magic. Yet the brain is not the object of worship, sitting anonymously near the sodas, lapping in its formaldehyde, blurred by the Tupperware. In fact, everyone seems utterly unaware of it, including its keeper. No, the man of the moment is Harvey, who dervishes through the crowd receiving his fans, tingling with handshakes, heady on the sweet perfume of social studies teachers.

"I'm meeting a footnote here," says one tall woman looking down at him. "And the kids are getting a chance to touch history." A student approaches, a sophomore, he says, by way of introduction, and asks Harvey whether he thinks it was a crock that Einstein didn't win the Nobel prize for relativity. "I mean, the photoelectric effect, give me a break," he says, and then cites various facts and stats of Einstein's life in the way that, when I was his age, I might have done with the Yankees' lineup. Harvey makes a show of deep consideration but then offers no opinion of his own.

Among these people, Harvey refers to himself without hesitation as a research scientist, and these people without hesitation take him at his word. For my part, I get cornered by an overly focused physics teacher who is intent on knowing my title. "What's your vector in all this?" he inquires. With cockeyed ferocity, he pegs me for Harvey's grandson, his agent, his bodyguard, his "AV man." I tell him that I'm just doing the driving. "Okay, yeah, let me get this straight," he says. "You drove him to California. Do you get union wages for that? Do you get extra for the brain?"

Harvey delivers his lecture in a dim, egg-cavern room flooded with students and the smell of bubble gum. Some wear baggy Starter sweats or jeans pulled low off their hips or unlaced high-tops; some have pierced noses or tongues or eyebrows. They are white and Asian and Latino and African American. A number of boys have shaved the sides of their head and wear mop-tops or Egyptian pharaoh 'dos; a number of the girls have dyed hair, all colors of the rainbow.

The teachers shush everyone, but the hormonal thrum defies complete silence, and there's a low-level sputter of laughter like a car chuffing even after the ignition's been turned off. I sit with Sarah Gonzalez about half way back and to the side. And then suddenly she stands, pats her hair, and makes her way to the podium to introduce Harvey, the gold of her glasses flashing success. Harvey, shaped like a black question mark, shambles to the front of the room, looking every bit the retired undertaker. There's scattered applause but the truth is that no one seems to care. Harvey places the Tupperware container on a table next to the lectern and clears his throat, chuckles, then clears his throat again. He runs his hands up and down the side of the podium, touches the Tupperware once with his finger, then focuses on a spot at the back of the room, rheumy-eyed, squinting. These are the thirteen-, fourteen-, and fifteen-year-olds of America—hundreds of clear eyes reflecting back at him, brains obsessed with boyfriends and girlfriends, band practice and basketball, sitcoms and rap stars—and Harvey, truly an old man now, seems at a loss. He begins a droning, discombobulated, start-and-stop remembrance of Albert Einstein, almost as if he's talking to himself.

"The great scientist would eventually come up with the equation $E=mc^2$, and how he did that I'll never know, heh-heh. . . .

"He was a friendly person. Real easy to talk to, you know. Wore flannels and tennis shoes a lot . . .

"I was just real lucky to be at the right place at the right time. . . ."

Einstein's doughy, animated face is flashed on a screen, Harvey's impassive one beneath it. When Harvey senses he's losing his audience, when he's on the verge of bombing, he tells them about the end of Einstein's life, about how Einstein knew five years prior to his death that he was dying but adamantly refused an operation. He tells them how even on the night he died he called for a pencil and paper, working one last time on his unified field theory, convinced perhaps that it was still within his grasp. Harvey tells them about the autopsy, about coming to the morgue that Monday morning to find the Great Scientist lying on the table, about how he did the autopsy and removed Einstein's brain. "He liked the fatty foods, you know," says Harvey. "That's what he died of." He starts slowly for the Tupperware and the entire audience, students and teachers, all lean forward in their seats, crane their necks, hold their collective breath. For the first time, there is complete silence.

He pops the lid and unabashedly fishes around for some of the brain, then holds up a chunk of it. It's almost like a dream—illogically logical, shockingly normal. My first real glimpse of the Tupperwared brain, and it is with three hundred teenage strangers. And I can barely see it! One girl squeals, and general chaotic murmurings fill the room. Kids come to their feet in waves of oohs and ahs. Someone in the back lets out an uncontrollable "Yo!" The smell of formaldehyde wafts thickly over them, a scent of the ages, and drives them back on their heels.

Harvey natters on, but no one is really listening now, just gasping at these blobs of brain. "I took the meninges off. . . . This is a little bit of the cortex. . . . He had more glial cells than the rest of us—those are the cells that nourish the neurons. . . ."

They are transfixed by the pale slices as if it were all a macabre Halloween joke. They're repulsed and captivated by the man whose fingers are wet with brain. Sarah Gonzalez stands up, slightly disheveled, flushed in the face. "Children, questions! Ask Dr. Harvey your questions!"

One swaggering boy in the back of the room raises his hand, seemingly offended: "Yeah, but like, WHAT'S THE POINT?"

Harvey doesn't hear, puts his hand behind his ear to signal that he doesn't hear, and a teacher sitting nearby translates: "He wants to know what the point is," says the teacher politely.

Harvey hesitates for a second, then almost seems angry. "To see the difference between your brain and a genius's," he shoots back.

The crowd titters. A girl throws a high five at her best friend. "Dang, girl."

The old man is cool!

Another boy in the back stands. "I was told, like, Einstein didn't want people to take his brain."

Again the teacher translates, and as soon as Harvey processes the question he bristles.

"Where are you getting your information?" he says.

"My world-government teacher," the boy says.

Harvey ponders this, then responds, as if it's answer enough. "In Germany, it's very common to do an autopsy and take the brain out."

When the period ends, the students storm Harvey and the brain. They want to know how long he's had it ("Since before your parents were born"). If he plans to clone it ("Way-ell, under the right conditions someday, I suppose it might be done"). Whether an evil dictator such as Saddam Hussein might try to get his hands on it ("Heh-heh-heh"). I try to get close, but the crowd is too thick, the crush to see the brain too great, and so I stand on the edges with Gonzalez, chatting, in a dull state of shock. Even as Harvey gambols outside later, a few students linger and a boy says, "Yo, man, where you going next? Can we follow?" Harvey flushes with triumph, stammers that he doesn't really know, as Sarah Gonzalez leads him to a seat in a waiting golf cart.

When we pull away, I wonder what we must look like to the students waving good-bye. Harvey rides shotgun as always, with the Tupperwared brain on his lap—a man beyond their own grandfathers, someone from a different dimension in space and time, really, lit down here for a weird moment at Independence High, telling tales about a zany-haired geek who supposedly changed the world. Then he's away again, vanishing on a golf cart down the concrete superstring sidewalks of their world.

19 ◆ The End of the Road

The finality of death took five years. Einstein's aneurysm had been diagnosed as early as 1950, and when doctors informed him that an operation might save his life, he said, "Let it burst." Like Newton before his own death, Einstein was less worried about his physical demise than the constant nagging doubts about his theories. "There is not a single concept of which I am convinced that it will stand firm," he wrote to an old friend, Maurice Solovine, in 1949, "and I feel uncertain whether I am in general on the right track." And while his brain kept whirring with the problems of a unified theory, his body became frail and thin, wrinkles fell over him like elephant skin, and he began to slouch, as if with each new day he was carrying a slightly heavier pack on his back. "The strange thing about growing old is that the intimate identification with the here and now is slowly lost," he wrote to the Queen Mother of Belgium in 1953, "one feels transposed into infinity, more or less alone, no longer in hope or fear, only observing."

On April 11, 1955, Einstein had a bad bellyache. He became dizzy and lost his appetite. But still he wouldn't let a doctor near him for two days, and then one was summoned only after he collapsed on the way to the bathroom. The doctor arrived at 112 Mercer Street, set up an electrocardiogram, and gave Einstein morphine to help get him through the night. His secretary, Helen Dukas, spoon-fed him ice cubes. He felt a bit better, but then he was struck again by crippling waves of pain that finally persuaded him to go to the hospital, where he immediately called on Dukas to bring his reading glasses and his work. On a Sunday, his son Hans Albert arrived and they talked for a while about various scientific matters. He saw his stepdaughter, Margot, too. "Do not let the house become a museum," he told her.

And just as the doctor felt the aneurysm might be repairing itself, Einstein worsened. Again, morphine. He slept peacefully until sometime after midnight, on into the early morning hours of April 18, when a nurse noticed his breathing had changed, as if the room suddenly had no oxygen. Panicked, she cranked up the head of the bed, and the old man muttered something in German, a language she didn't understand. Then he simply stopped breathing.

I think about these last mortal moments—about Einstein's abiding doubt in his own theories and how he worked until the end, his last page of calculations written in such a scrunched, neat hand and yet so inscrutable, like a Pali inscription. I think about his last afternoon alive, the appearance of his son and stepdaughter, of those few people closest to him. And how all of those final good-byes were treated in such a mundane, seemingly impersonal way. No deathbed confessions. No final epiphany. No mention of the people not there, those to whom he'd once professed his love: Mileva, Elsa, his institutionalized son, Eduard. And what finally did he mumble in German before he departed his own body and left it there for Dr. Thomas Stoltz Harvey?

I think about this on the brightest day of our strange trip, as light pours over northern California—overflowing the hollows and flatland, gathering to the leaves of trees, bathing the buildings of Oakland and San Francisco, and flashing from every window. Harvey seems to catch flame sitting next to me. He is now eight years older than the physicist when he died. How much longer does he have? "The devil altogether counts the years conscientiously, one's got to acknowledge that," said Einstein. And I think about my grandfather, who didn't believe in heaven or hell—and who denied to himself that there would be an end at all. And my parents, whose end I can't imagine. And then, of course, me, the one trying to find a reason for living in the first place.

I think of Sara when I last saw her, saying good-bye at the bus. And I reconstruct that moment, particle by particle. The frigid snowfall. The gray sky. The chill of winter and the million frozen molecules between us. I had wanted to leave. I wanted my freedom, to be set loose in the world—unstrung, unburdened, and young. But, out in America, time bends and comes around on itself, the young become old, and the old young again. The farther we travel from each other, the closer we become. And suddenly on this stretch of California highway, I'm back at that Maine bus station with Sara bundled in wool, and our dog licking the ice between us on the curb. And this time I don't want to go.

⚛

Albert Einstein's granddaughter, Evelyn, greets us at the door to her upscale Berkeley apartment complex, in a black jumper, wearing two *Star Trek* pins and globe earrings. Nearly a head taller than Harvey, she is a big-boned fifty-six-year-old, though she looks younger, with a short bob of brown hair. Due to the fact that she has cancer and a failing liver, she walks in small steps and breathes heavily after the slightest exertion. She gives off an aura of enormous sadness, though her powers of humor and forgiveness seem to run equally as deep. Despite the distress that Harvey's removal of the brain caused her father—who died in 1973 of a heart attack at the age of sixty-nine—she has invited him to her house.

While Evelyn is allegedly the adopted daughter of Hans Albert, the circumstance of her lineage is a bit clouded. Acting on the suggestion that Evelyn might actually be Albert's daughter from an affair with a New York dancer, one of the researchers who studied Einstein's brain, Dr. Charles Boyd, tried to match the DNA of Albert's brain matter and Evelyn's skin. And although Albert's DNA was too denatured to decipher, the experiment led to something of a row. Even as Evelyn characterizes Boyd's theory as "unfortunate and unfounded," her resemblance to Einstein, the mirthful play of light in her heavy-lidded eyes and the Picasso shape of her face, is uncanny. Evelyn herself ruefully says, "If you believe in what Albert said about time, then I'm really his grandmother anyway."

From her light-filled living room, we can see the skyline of San Francisco, Angel Island rising from the sun-flecked blue bay; Mt. Tamalpais lurking in the distance. It's a lovely spot. Among artifacts and antique clocks, Evelyn offers us seats. We've come a long way and yet it feels as if Harvey would like to be anywhere else but here. Evelyn sits down. I fall onto the plush couch. Harvey remains standing.

Evelyn tells us about what it was like to grow up as an Einstein, how her life became an exercise in navigating the jagged shoals of her family. Her father had inherited a degree of his own father's cold distance—she refers to her grandfather only as "Albert" or "Albie"—and Evelyn found herself shipped off to school in Switzerland, where she occasionally visited her uncle Eduard at the institution where he lived. She came back to Berkeley for college, had a bad marriage, went through a difficult time during which she says she lived on the streets for a year, then later worked as a cop here, trolling the waterfront on a mountain bike, and then moved on to deprogramming cult members. Now, she seems to live in relative comfort, though she has very few keepsakes from her grandfather. She claims that most of the letters he'd once sent to her were stolen.

As she speaks, Harvey still stands frozen in the middle of the room, much like a squirrel on the first branch of a tree above two barking hounds. Evelyn does what she can to politely ignore him, asks me innocuous questions about the trip, waiting for him to sit, too. But he doesn't. He's just glued there, the Tupperwared brain in his trembling hands. He breathes more quickly. Somewhere in his head, I picture virulent, radioactive cells of guilt proliferating. And he just won't sit. Having arrived here, does he now have second thoughts? Could he ever have imagined, those four decades ago, when he cut the brain from Einstein's head, that he would now be standing here before Evelyn Einstein with it in his hands?

The fourth time that Evelyn offers him a seat he takes it. He laughs nervously, then clears his throat. "Real good," he says. Evelyn is talking some more about cults, how it's the Scientologists who scare her most, how easy the cult business really is—and how sinister. "All my friends say I should start one and we could become multimillionaires," she says, joking. "I could channel Albert. I mean, when Linda Evans channels Ramtha she talks like Yul Brynner. It's just hysterical. If this broad can channel a thirty-thousand-year-old guy, I can channel Albert."

At that, Harvey abruptly pulls out a sheaf of photographs and slides with cresyl violet stains of axons and glial cells, then plunks the Tupperware on the table. "Ah, brain time," says Evelyn, and Harvey just begins a lecture as if he's talking to the youngsters at Independence High School again, still wearing his black undertaker's suit. "This is a picture of the brain from different aspects, olfactory nerve, and so forth." He pulls out a photo of Einstein. "I like this picture because it shows him as a younger man, you know, when he first came over to be an American. So many of the photos you see of him are when he was an older man."

"I have a lot when he was young," says Evelyn.

"You do? I'll trade you some," says Harvey.

"Did you autopsy the whole body?"

"The whole body."

"What was that like?"

Harvey pauses a moment, clears his throat. "Why, it made me feel humble and insignificant."

"Did he have a gallbladder? Or had they taken it out?"

"I think he still had a gallbladder. Heh-heh. Yeah, his diet was his nemesis, you know, because he lived before we knew what cholesterol did to the blood, so he probably walked around with high blood cholesterol, much of it being deposited in his blood vessels. That aorta, that was just full of cholesterol plaque."

Evelyn nods. "Yeah . . . well, of course, the European diet. My father and I would fight over fat. When we got a ham, we would cut off the fat and fry it, then fight over it. Bitterly." Evelyn smiles.

"And all that good goose grease," chimes in Harvey.

"Oh yeah. Well, in those days goose . . . well, goose is actually a lot safer than beef, a lot less cholesterol."

"Oh yeah? I didn't know that."

"It's a family that just adored fat," she says.

"I used to eat in a little inn up in Metuchen, New Jersey, where your grandfather would spend weekends, and they had these cheeses, you know, full-fat cheeses and nice wines."

"I don't know if he was into wines," says Evelyn.

"I never saw him drink it myself," says Harvey, forgetting, then perhaps remembering, that he met Einstein only once, briefly in passing, to take his blood. "Well, the innkeeper had a good supply of wine, and I thought it was for your grandfather. Maybe it wasn't."

There is some talk about the size of the brain. Evelyn contends that at 2.7 pounds it qualifies as microcephalic according to the 1923 edition of *Gray's Anatomy*—that is, smaller than normal—but Harvey insists that the brain was normal size for a man Einstein's age, given the fact that brains shrink over time. He lets her see some slides but seems unwilling to open the Tupperware. When I ask him if he'd show us pieces of the brain, he seems a bit put out, uncaps the lid for a moment, then almost immediately lids it again. Still, he verbally offers Evelyn a piece—to which she says, "That would be wonderful"—then, curiously, never gives it to her. Evelyn looks as perplexed as I am. After all of this, after offering it for perusal to scores of total strangers, it seems Harvey has decided that there will be no show-and-tell with the actual gray matter.

"I'm amazed they didn't work with the brain earlier, right away when he died, actually," Evelyn says. Though she's aware of the controversies that plagued Harvey, she doesn't press him. Still, the old man stiffens into his pillar of salt. The words slow as they come from his mouth: something about the fissure of Sylvius, occipital lobe, cingulate gyrus. All of it a part of some abstract painting, some hocus-pocus act. "It took us a while," he says finally.

As we begin to make plans for dinner, Harvey abruptly ends the meeting. "Well, it's been a real play-sure," he says, taking us both by surprise. And then he explains: Earlier, in San Jose—and once again, unbeknownst to me—he made a call to his eighty-five-year-old cousin in San Mateo and now insists that he must go spend the night there, assuming that I will take him more than halfway back to San Jose in rush-hour traffic. But to come this far for only half an hour? And besides, Evelyn has made reservations for us all to have dinner. But nothing sways Harvey. "I think I have to go," he says. "I promised." I suggest that his cousin join us or that we visit his cousin in the morning after rush hour. Harvey stands firm. "Way-ell now, I'm going." Then I stand firm. "I'm staying." After four thousand miles of driving, I, for one, am eating with Evelyn Einstein. Harvey gets on the phone with his cousin and says loudly enough so that I can hear, "The chauffeur won't give me a ride."

Harvey decides to take public transportation—BART—and then have his cousin pick him up at the station. And so he does. We pile into the Skylark and drive to a nearby station, Harvey in the back-seat with the brain. Evelyn uses these last minutes to try to clarify something that still bugs her: the presence of Otto Nathan, Einstein's executor, at the autopsy. As it turns out, according to Evelyn, Nathan and Helen Dukas, didn't treat Hans Albert well at all after Einstein's death, and the bad blood continues to this day,

though both are dead now, too. But Harvey doesn't seem to listen,
makes random small talk.

Don't know much about this fella, O. J. Simpson, heh-heh,
And I don't understand what he had for cut-up bodies,
But one trial says he's innocent; and the other says he's guilty.
As if he owned Albie. They say he even sprinkled his ashes.
Justice? I wish there'd been more Negroes on the jury.

When we come to the BART station and Harvey begins to collect
his stuff, it suddenly occurs to me that this is it, the first time in
eleven days that we'll be separated. Though we'll meet again tomorrow for a friendly visit with the brain researcher, Marian Diamond,
whose work was long ago finished on Einstein's brain, this feels like
the real end to our journey. And it's so abrupt that, at first, I don't feel
anything but the wrongness of Harvey leaving my side.

In the backseat of the Skylark now, Harvey opens his case and
presents Evelyn with a postcard: the black-and-white photo of himself looking pensive in a striped turtleneck, his ear the size of a small
slipper, gazing sleepy-eyed at some form in the distance, some
ghostly presence. "That's a very nice one," she says politely.

"Yessir," says Harvey. "Couldn't have been happier to meet . . ."

It all seems so anticlimactic, but so appropriate. So like Harvey.
Tomorrow, when we say our last good-bye, it will be virtually the
same. We'll stand among a funky, rainbow-coalition of Berkeley students, Harvey with his plaid suitcase in hand and black Wallabees on
his feet, on his way back to visit his cousin—and then to fly home to
Cleora. And me, on my way to visit friends in San Francisco and then
to wait for Sara's arrival and a few days of vacation together. I'll think
to hug him good-bye but then we'll only shake hands. A young man
and an old man. A chauffeur and his passenger. I guess friends, of a
curious sort.

With Evelyn and I watching him from the car now, he shuffles slowly toward the BART entrance, suitcase full of cellophane-wrapped clothes. I feel a pang then, seeing him caught up in a river of people drifting toward the escalators. He suddenly seems very small and vulnerable, his full eighty-four years, spilling underground, the silver tassel of his hair flashing once. Then his body goes down, vanishing in the catacomb's shadow.

⚛

Evelyn and I drive north of Berkeley to the Hotel Mac for dinner. We share some wine and a delicious meal of salmon and tenderloin. We take our time, linger for almost three hours. I listen to Evelyn as she tells about the terribly complex legal battle she's waged against her nephew Thomas and an attorney named Michael Ferguson. According to Evelyn, her stepmother Elizabeth, Hans Albert's second wife, had set up the Albert Einstein Correspondence Trust, which included approximately four hundred of the physicist's personal papers. Evelyn claimed she was never informed that she was a beneficiary of the trust, so she sued to seek a share of the documents. The lawsuit was eventually settled. "It's not so easy being an Einstein," Evelyn says. "When I was going to school at Berkeley in the sixties, I could never tell if men wanted to be with me because of me, or my name. To say, you know, I had an Einstein."

It's not until we get back in the car that something catches my eye, sitting on the backseat, lit by a streetlight. I stare at it for a moment, but it doesn't seem possible. It looks like a Tupperware container. It *is* a Tupperware container! The brain! I'm dumbfounded, as is Evelyn. It seems unfathomable that Harvey would have forgotten it, but then maybe not. Perhaps it's the thing Harvey's been working up to, but hasn't known how to execute, this parting with the brain. Which would explain his awkwardness, his near rudeness, with Evelyn and me.

"He left the brain?" says Evelyn, still incredulous. "Does he do this often?"

"Nope," I say, and suddenly we are smiling at each other.

We don't look at it right away—right there in full view of the strolling sidewalk masses—but drive back to Evelyn's apartment by the bay. I stop in front of the building with the Skylark idling. I reach back and take the Tupperware in my hands, and by the dome light of the car, open the container.

After all these miles, all these days on the road, after finally having given up on this moment, it's here. Chunks of Einstein's brain are pouched in a white cloth, floating in their broth. I lift the lid, unravel a swath of damp cloth, and then maybe a dozen golf-ball-size chunks of the brain spill out—parts from the cerebral cortex and the frontal lobe. The smell of formaldehyde smacks us like a backhand, and for a moment I actually feel as if I might puke. The pieces are sealed in celloidin—the pinkish, liver-colored blobs of brain rimmed by gold wax. I pick some out of the plastic container and hand a few to Evelyn. They feel squishy, weigh about the same as very light beach stones. We hold them up like jewelers, marveling at how they seem less like a brain than—what?—some kind of snack food, some kind of energy chunk for genius triathletes. Or an edible product that offers the consumer world peace, space travel, eternity. Even today, the Asmat of Irian Jaya believe that to consume a brain is to gain the mystical essence of another person; and Microsoft employees glug potions of herbal energy elixirs called Einstein's Brain at company parties. But to be absolutely honest, I never thought that, holding Einstein's brain, I'd somehow imagine eating it.

"So this is what all the fuss is about?" says Evelyn. She pokes at the brain nuggets still in the Tupperware, laps formaldehyde on them. A security guard walks by and glances at us, then keeps walking. There is, I must admit, something entirely surreal about Evelyn messing around with her grandfather's brain, checking his soggy neurons. But she seems more intrigued than grossed out. "You could make a nice necklace of this one," she says, holding up a circular piece of brain. "This is pretty weird, huh?"

Watching her in the cast of thin light—an impression of her sadness returning to me, the thrill of adrenaline confusing everything—I'm overcome with a desire to make her happy for a moment. Without thinking, I say, "You should take it." Then I remind her that Harvey had offered her a piece earlier but had never given it to her. "It belongs to you anyway," I say. Weeks later, on the phone, she'll tell me, "I wish I'd taken it." But now, sitting back in the teal velour of the Skylark, she sighs and says, "I couldn't."

Instead, she puts the pieces back in the Tupperware, closes it, and hands it to me. She gets out of the car and heavily walks herself inside.

Which leaves just me and the brain.

20 ◆ Mr. Albert and Me

We—the brain and I—drive the East Shore Freeway to University Avenue. We skirt the bay, all black and glassed-over, San Francisco on the other side like so many lit-up missile silos—and then head toward Shattuck Avenue. Although I'm exhausted, I suddenly feel very free, have this giddy desire to start driving back across America, without Harvey, without anyone. Just me—and the brain. Maybe I'd take it home, put it on the mantel. I like to think now that somehow Sara would understand. On the radio, there's a local talk show about UFOs, an expert insisting that in February 1954, Eisenhower disappeared for three days, allegedly making contact with aliens.

Why not? Anything seems possible now.

We soon find that all the hotels and motels in Berkeley are full. Every place but the Flamingo Motel—a pink, concrete, L-shaped, forties-style two-story with a mod neon rendering of a flamingo. A fleabag. But it's enough. A double bed, a bathroom, a rotary phone. Some brother partyers have an upstairs room at the far end of the motel and are drinking cases of Pabst Blue Ribbon. As I carry the brain up to my room, they eye me, then hoot and toss their crushed cans over the banister into the parking lot.

"Whatta moon!" I say to no one but the brain. And it is quite a moon, big and orange.

When I open the door, we're hit with a wallop of disinfectant. The room itself is the size of a couple of horse stalls, with a rust-colored unvacuumed shag rug scorched with cigarette burns. A few stations come in on the television, which is bolted high on the wall. *Nightline* is getting to the bottom of the cloning business. It's been a long day, and yet the brain has got me pumped up. I try to make a call—try Sara—but the phone is broken. I think to send a few postcards, to my brothers maybe, but my pen explodes. By some trick of the room's mirror, it seems that there are lights levitating everywhere, but they are strangely comforting. Finally, not quite knowing what to do, I go to bed. I put Einstein's brain on one pillow and rest my own head on the other one next to it, six inches away. Just to see. I've come four thousand miles for this moment, and now all I suddenly want to do is sleep. Light from the road slips over the room—a greenish underwater glow—and the traffic noise dims. I can hear beer cans softly pattering down on the pavement, then nothing.

It's possible that in our dreams we enter a different dimension of the universe. On this night, it's possible that I suddenly have three wives, ten kids, and twelve grandchildren, that I've become Harvey himself, that I open up bodies to find more bodies and open those bodies to find that I'm falling through space and time. It's possible that, in some fifth dimension, I'm Robert Oppenheimer and Mahatma Gandhi, Billie Holiday and Thurman Munson. I'm Navajo and Dinka. I'm Tupac Amaru and a NASA astronaut. Or that my name is Kenji or Joseph, that I'm a scatterling or a person in a field in North Dakota about to be abducted by a UFO. It's possible, too, that I'm nobody, or rather only myself, slightly dazed and confused, far away from home, curled in a question mark in a pink motel with Einstein's brain on the pillow by my head, waiting to wake up to who I am.

Soon the sun is blasting back through the Flamingo's cheap drapes. Morning, and I'm craving orange juice. And, too, the world is as I left it—the desk chair in its place, the wrapped soap in the shower, the brain sitting demurely on its pillow, the Flamingo still the Flamingo, with cigarette burns in the rusty rug. Yet there's a sudden grand beauty to its shoddiness. When I step outside into the bright, early-morning sun of California, I have the top off the Tupperware. And although later in the day, when we meet again, I will return the brain to Harvey without one morsel of regret—and he will take it from me without any acknowledgment whatsoever—I am for a brief moment the man with the plan, the keeper of the cosmos. Do I feel the thing that relics, totems, and fetishes are supposed to make people feel? Something that I can believe in? A power larger than myself that I can submit to? Salvation? Have I touched eternity?

I'm not sure. The beer cans strewn in the parking lot make out the rough shape of America, surrounded by pools of sudsy gold liquid. And the birds have come down out of the sky and they're drinking from it. Even now, the universe is filling with dark matter. We're slowing down. Snowballs the size of jumbo trucks are pelting our atmosphere. Perhaps a meteor has just been bumped into a new flight pattern, straight toward Earth, and we won't know anything about it until it explodes us all, as meteors once exploded the dinosaurs.

But I am here now. In the now now. Day has come back up from the other side of the earth, the birds have come down from the sky. There are flashes of orange light, the air is flooded with honeysuckle. I feel something I can't quite put my finger on, something euphoric but deeply unsayable. Is it love or just not hate? Is it joy or just not sadness? For a moment, all of time seems to flow through the Flamingo, its bright edges reflecting the past and the present, travelers packing their bags and rivering into some further future. We are always driving with our secrets in the trunk, amazed by the cows and rainbows and palm trees. And do I dare to think that there will be no ending of the world, of America, of ourselves? I do. I really do. For in some recurrence, in some light wave, in some shimmer of time, we are out there now, and forever, existing, even as surely as Einstein himself continues to exist, here in my hands.

Afterword • The Unified Field Theory of Shad

Early spring, and smoke billows from chimneys. Deer loiter beneath cindered clouds on the icy edge of New Jersey lawns. In the year since our road trip, Harvey and I have talked on the phone, promised visits, but life has intervened. Harvey has been to Greece, to vacation with his former roommate Archie's family, spending a wonderful time with all of them, including Archie's grandmother. Sadly, his sister has recently passed away, and Cleora, his girlfriend, has broken her hip.

Sara and I have now been together for seven years. Some months ago Sara's mother died in a scuba diving accident. On one of the murky nights just after, lying sleeplessly in Sara's childhood bed, in her childhood home, we realized that there were so many things we hadn't yet known about her: She could read braille; she knew how to speak Navajo; she was a friend to underdogs and losers and anyone, really, whom she met.

"What if I forget her voice?" Sara said.

"You won't," I said. "You sound just like her."

In the months to come, we'll buy a house together and get married and have a son—all of it occurring so naturally that we won't even think of ourselves as having given up our freedom, but rather as having more of it. And we won't think of ourselves as having grown that much older, but as that much younger. Now, I'm driving one clear lane through New Jersey at twilight. On my way to Harvey—and Einstein's brain. Again.

Up around a bend, over a hill, and then there's the 1950s ranch. No sooner have I pulled in than Harvey is clip-clopping down the concrete steps. He's wearing a navy-blue sweater and blue turtleneck and blue jeans. Mr. Blue—beaming. "Yessir, real good to see you," he says. He holds my hand tightly, pulls himself close, then fades by (his shorter leg again). Cleora is there, too, struggling a bit with her injury, taking a bone strengthener called Fosamax, but generally in fine spirits and determined to be the consummate hostess she is. I forgot how kind a face she has. We climb back up the stairs together, then Harvey shuttles down again to fetch Cleora—"Okay, sweetie," he says, taking her arm—and then all of us squeeze through the door into the kitchen.

There's so much news to catch up on that no one knows where to begin, and for a while silence reigns. "Tom, why don't you two go sit in the living room?" Cleora says. And so we do, among glass trinkets and hooked rugs and a big, sculpted head of Cleora. Harvey seems exactly the same to me, except for one nod to age and humility: a hearing aid that he now wears in one of his ears.

We sit for a while, listening to the clock, and then Harvey starts talking about shad. The fish. He tells me about a magnificent shad festival once held in these parts, in Lawrenceville, and it recalls for him another era on the Connecticut River back up there in Connecticut, during his days at Yale, when shad parties were commonplace and shad was placed on boards and grilled over fires and people of all stripes ate lots of shad. These times of shad come tumbling into the room as mouthwateringly good memories, though when I ask Harvey what shad actually tastes like, he says, "Don't know. Never had it." Then we sit some more. Finally, I say, "Hey, you wanna go get some food?" And Harvey brightens and says, "Why sure. That'd be real nice."

Cleora stays at home, resting. Harvey and I hit one of his favorites,

Lieggi's, a throwback to the restaurants of yore when dark-wood paneling and good flatware signaled haute cuisine to the ritzy people of Trenton. It's a place that probably recorded its best days in 1950 and stays in business now on the greenbacks and Jacksons of a more gentrified, geezerly crowd. When we arrive, a handful sit scattered at their habitual tables, studying the same stained menus, fiddling wrinkled fingers on the same stained tablecloths from decades before. Our waiter sternly bustles around us, mumbling the day's specials in decibels so low that when Harvey, hand to ear, asks for "a repeat," the waiter takes the opportunity to exhale loudly and then virtually yells them back. "Sure has some pipes," says Harvey when he departs. Then he chuckles, a sweet sound tumble-drying over itself.

Thus follows the usual, prolonged consideration of the menu by Harvey. And where he once might have frustrated me—surveying, ordering, amending, surveying again—I cheerfully announce to our unamused waiter that I will have whatever my friend has, then prop my hands behind my head and relax. Harvey finally orders scrod and a bottle of the Australian "shi-razzz." And then we drift back to more Harvey memories, from a time before the brain. In an upcoming paper to be published in a British medical journal, *The Lancet*, Dr. Sandra Witelson and her Canadian colleagues will find that Einstein's inferior parietal lobe, the region that governs mathematical ability and spatial reasoning, is 15 percent larger than normal, while his Sylvian fissure is much smaller than average, suggesting an interconnection of neurons that may have allowed the scientist's brain to work more effectively. Though this paper will offer Harvey a kind of vindication, making headlines around the world, it will also raise more questions than it answers.

"Her study is simplistic," says Dr. Elliot Krauss, the man who holds the position Harvey himself once held at Princeton Hospital. "It's one step away from phrenology. You know, the ancient study of bumps on a head."

But now the brain seems curiously absent. Harvey again recalls the year he spent in a sanatorium while in med school at Yale, his tuberculosis, the inflammation of his lungs. He describes how at that time, in severe cases of pleurisy, doctors would actually break the rib cage in order to subdue the lungs. He recalls playing chess and reading a lot and just sitting around, staring out the window. And he remembers a friend who died there—and how when he, Thomas Stoltz Harvey, came out of that sanatorium, no one really remembered him.

After dinner, we go back to Cleora's house and sit again in the living room, in antique chairs, sipping bourbon. Harvey is talking football, old-time football. "Whatta scatback, that Albie Booth!" he says. When he talks about Albie Booth, it's like a code, opening another door to his past, for running right there beside the great back of yesteryear, breaking downfield in his imagination with the same fleet-footed ballet, is Harvey himself, perhaps in his mind a sleeker Harvey, a smarter Harvey, a more successful Harvey, a sexier Harvey, a more quintessentially Ivy Harvey who brings the crowd to its feet in New Haven's Yale Bowl. And running downfield in that frozen moment, too, is the possible Harvey—everything that he was before the brain, everything that he had perhaps hoped for himself before he became a pathologist checking under the hood of a lot of dead bodies, a father helping to raise a family—then another and another. And increasingly: a seeming spectator in his own life.

Now, it's way past his bedtime. He yawns, heavy-lidded, but still tries to keep himself up. He removes his glasses and rubs his eyes, and for a second the once-strapping man of Montgomery Clift good looks seems much older somehow—and unburdened. Only the next day do I come to understand why.

In the morning, I wake on a chintz couch in the basement, wrapped in crocheted blankets, among blown glass and seashells, oil lamps and candles. When I go upstairs, Cleora has set grapefruit and cereal on the table for all of us. I've planned to visit Princeton Hospital this morning, to see the morgue where Einstein's autopsy took place, and secretly hope that Harvey might accompany me. But he demurs. "I think you're going to have a real interesting day," he says cryptically, then says no more. When the time comes, he ushers me to the door. There's no official good-bye. Harvey just clasps my hand again and smiles. "Yessir," he says. "Yessir."

"Yessir," I say in return, and we leave it right there.

I drive back roads to the hospital to meet Elliot Krauss. Today the hospital is a modern state-of-the-art facility, catering to all the sundry gallstones and faulty ventricles of Princeton's rich, famous, and ridiculously smart. A tallish, forty-something man with a salt-and-pepper mustache, Krauss lurks in the basement of the hospital, among the water pipes and wires, hidden away where people can't mistakenly walk in on a body being autopsied. When we meet in the lobby, he says he has a surprise for me.

But first he takes me to the autopsy room, which is almost exactly the same today as it was back in 1955 when Einstein himself was rolled in: a small, brightly lit place with light green tile walls, huge sucking vents, a big refrigerator for bodies, and a bug zapper ("Yes," he says when I look at the zapper, "you don't know how much flies love a body until you work in a morgue"). Near the autopsy table is the scale bearing the name Chatillon. There are vacuums and water hoses and silver bowls in which the organ tree is dumped, the liver and lungs and heart and kidneys. In one closet there are a number of hanging brains, fixed in formaldehyde. His morgue assistant, called a diener, is a large African-American man who until recently had to wrestle bodies from the freezer to the table himself. Now the hospital has a forklift that does the trick.

Krauss tells me that on the day of Einstein's death, after Harvey did the autopsy, the people of Princeton Hospital put aside their differences for a moment and lined up to see the Great One's body in the morgue, marching in and out all day long, in hushed wonderment.

"I think Harvey has gotten a bit of a bum rap," Krauss says. "Many,

many people were interested in Einstein's body after he died. But then all pathologists get bad raps. I mean, everyone thinks we're down here all day digging through corpses, but that's a small part of the job. You know when tissue gets removed during a biopsy?" Krauss doesn't wait for my answer. "Well, that's us! That's our job down here—to analyze it for cancer or whatever. But we don't get credit for it. Everyone thinks their doctor did it and sometimes you get doctors who act like they did—but it's the pathologist."

Krauss leads me back to his windowless office, offers me a seat, then sits down and becomes very serious. He lets a delicious beat of suspense pass between us. "You want to see something?" he asks, drumming a pencil on his desk. "Why not," I say. Krauss smiles and reaches under his desk. He struggles for a moment with something large, a cardboard box holding something heavy that he lifts from the floor and sets atop the charts and paperwork strewn before him. When he puts it on the desk, it shudders from the weight of the contents.

"Do you know what this is?" he asks. It's a rhetorical question, but now, doing a quick calculation, figuring that Krauss is a veteran body-parts man who by this stage in his career probably doesn't get worked up by too much, I'm suddenly of the mind that perhaps I'm underestimating this moment. Perhaps Krauss himself has some terrible, speckled secret, some strange appendage, or three-headed freak fetus he wants to spring on me. I squint in that don't-show-me, show-me way of squinting and then he reaches in and delicately handles an object. Out of the box comes a glass cookie jar. He gently sets the jar in front of the box, then he produces another. Two cookie jars, sloshing and purling with chunks of . . . brain. "Einstein's brain!" he says, beaming. He stands back, hands on his hips, and gestures at the cookie jars like some kind of Vegas-act magician.

"But," I start, then stop. "I don't get it," I say. "What about Harvey?"

Krauss nods, then starts shaking his head. "I know," he says. "I know. It's unbelievable. Gave it to me two days ago. But we'd been talking for a long time and the talks turned into negotiations and Thomas Harvey wanted to make sure that the brain was put in the right hands, to keep the study alive."

"You?" I ask.

"Yes, me," says Krauss.

"But why? I mean this"—I point to the two jars of Einstein's brain—"is *him*."

"Well then, he's free now," says Krauss with a laugh. "And I'm shackled."

No wonder Harvey seemed so relaxed—no—so ethereal! In one act, he has rewound time. He has put the brain back into the hands of himself, reincarnated as Elliot Krauss, and then stepped aside—or stepped beyond. And here's Krauss, flushed and yammering excitedly. He tells me that his strategy is to protect the brain, keep it out of harm's way and hope that, with increased knowledge and technology, and despite a certain amount of denaturement, the brain will still one day yield important fruit of some kind. "What do you mean?" I say. "Clone another Einstein?"

"Why not?" says Krauss, smiling. "We may be able to recover the DNA."

"But do you really think . . . ?"

"What Tom Harvey did was attempt to preserve the greatest brain of the century," says Krauss. "In thirty years, it's possible that Einstein's brain won't be quite the curiosity it is right now, that we'll have the means to actually use it and understand its secrets. I think Harvey knows he's not going to get there with us. And so . . ." Krauss gestures again to the brain.

It seems impossible—or at the very least like a bit of news Harvey himself might have shared with me during our visit, rather than rhapsodizing about shad. But it's not betrayal or jealousy or anything of that petty humanly sort that I feel now. It's a little prick of electric pain around the edge of my heart because I'm suddenly imagining Harvey giving up the brain. I picture him on that last winding drive from his house to the hospital, Einstein's brain in the trunk for one final time. Perhaps he felt as he did on the day he first drove away with it. I imagine him cruising slowly, taking extra precaution and care, leaving on his blinkers long after he's actually turned.

Then I imagine him shuffling past the information desk, with the heavy cardboard box in hand, for he wouldn't have allowed anyone to do this part for him. I imagine him standing in the door frame to Krauss's office, knowing this is where the journey ends—right where it started. "What did he say to you?" I ask Krauss.

"He really didn't say anything. He just walked in here and handed me the cardboard box. I mean, I think he was relieved. He looked relieved, but he really didn't say anything. Didn't give me instructions or anything. And now it's mine."

He looks both elated and forlorn, jazzed and confused. "I can't keep it here," he says, wringing his hands, "because every time I leave this office I have a vision of returning and finding the brain gone. You know, maybe some innocent cleaning person just tossing it out or something. Or then maybe someone just stealing it because it's probably worth millions."

Talking to Krauss, I suddenly have the oddest sensation, a visitation, really. I believe that I'm hearing Harvey's voice, that Harvey is speaking to me from forty-five years ago, through this man. And he is telling me he is afraid, that he's in a spot because he didn't plan for Einstein's brain but that somehow he now possesses this holy object and is duty-bound to protect it. He knows his world will never be the same. When I ask Krauss where he plans to keep Einstein's brain, he looks at me hopelessly and again Harvey speaks. "I don't know— maybe I'll just take it home."

"Yeah, that's a good idea," I tell him.

It's late when I leave Princeton, heading west. The streetlights have come on and then soon I'm driving country roads again until I can find a freeway that sends me back home to Sara in Maine. There are a few crows pecking at fallow fields and the trees look like a very dark alphabet, letters from another world. When I think of Harvey, I imagine him driving home again, too—those first moments of freedom after relinquishing Einstein's brain. I imagine dinner that night with Cleora. After having had other husbands and wives, they're together, a certain gaiety and lightness between them, a fondness that is love and maybe a feeling rising up in Harvey that, after all, he really did belong to this one woman, to this one world.

Look there. The clock is ticking in Cleora's living room, and the pipes run with cold water. Yes, do you see that the wires are still alive with electricity? Even as this old man, Thomas Stoltz Harvey, creeps down the hall to the bedroom and strips naked before his Maker, even as he succumbs to a light snoring spell, driven down to sweet sleep by the moon falling through his window, can you see this old man now, carried up by his angels?

Acknowledgments

There are many people to whom I owe a debt of gratitude for this book. The first, of course, is Dr. Thomas Harvey, road warrior and uber-pilgrim, whose generosity and friendship I value as much as his sage advice that sometimes when on the road, a Wendy's baked potato is next to God.

Without *Harper's Magazine,* which published the original article that became this book, I would be painting houses. To Colin Harrison, friend and high priest who deciphered, organized, and collated my words and then sat at the Noho Star reading them back to me, I owe my second born. And to Lewis Lapham, benefactor-at-large, who provided the book's title, I owe my third. Thanks as well to everyone at the magazine, including Angela Riechers and Aida Edemariam, whose scrupulous fact-check of the original article was the catalyst for the fresh reporting in these pages.

My agent, Sloan Harris, is a deep-sea fisherman of the soul, and everything that he has done on behalf of this book leaves me humbled. I'm truly lucky to have such a friend.

At The Dial Press my editor, Susan Kamil, is a goddess who met every shred of authorial doubt with sparkling faith. Her unwavering patience and support, humor, and editorial insight carried this book to completion. In addition, I'm grateful to Leslie Hermsdorf, who first spotted a real book in this tale, to Carla Riccio, who also championed this project from the start, and to Zoë Rice, whose hard work and cheer have repeatedly buoyed the day.

In helping me research the book, Julie Greenberg went above and beyond the call of duty, and I thank her for her relentless curiosity and collaboration. As well as conducting several key interviews, she sent all kinds of odd brain goodies my way. In addition, I appreciate the time and insight offered by Nina Long at the Wistar Institute, Alice Calaprice at Princeton University Press, Robert Schulman and Michel Janssen of the Einstein Papers at Boston University, John Taylor at the National Archives, Dr. Johan Kosek and Dr. Sylvia Forno of Stanford University, Neal Singer of Sandia National Laboratory, Dr. Marian Diamond at University of California, Berkeley, and Kenji Sugimoto of Kinki University in Osaka, Japan, who sponsored two joyous days of reporting there.

Several journalists and filmmakers have set the stage for anyone hoping to tell the tale of Einstein's brain, so I owe a debt to Steven Levy of *Newsweek* for first finding Dr. Harvey, and Einstein's brain, and Gina Maranto for her reporting on the brain in *Discover* magazine. Kevin Hull's 1994 documentary, *Einstein's Brain*, is a masterpiece, and it is Hull who first discovered the existence of Einstein's eyes. I'm glad for his willingness to meet with me in England. When it came to the details of Albert Einstein's life, I enlisted help from a multitude of biographies, including those by Abraham Pais, Roger Highfield and Paul Carter, Ronald Clark, Banesh Hoffman, Brian Denis and Albrecht Folsing. Alice Calaprice's *The Quotable Einstein* also proved invaluable. In reporting on Hiroshima, I partially relied on accounts by Kenzaburo Oe and Richard Rhodes. My own path to Einstein's brain led through the late writer William Burroughs and his friend Steven Lowe, while James Grauerholz was instrumental in arranging a meeting with the writer.

Along the road we were met by all manner of friendliness and hospitality. For that I thank Cleora Wheatly, Roger Richman, Sarah Gonzalez and family, and Evelyn Einstein, whose generosity under trying circumstances was as commendable as it was inspiring. Scott Greenberg and Clare Hertel are guilty of being the best friends a traveler could ever hope to meet after two thousand miles—and also guilty of just being the best friends period.

In the course of writing this book I've relied on the support of many kind souls. At *Esquire* magazine, two of the very best, David Granger and Peter Griffin, have stood behind me from the get-go and to both of them, I'm very grateful—as I am to Jim Adams, and everyone else there. Will Dana, Doug Stanton, Elwood "Black Fly" Reid, Alyson Hagy, Bob

Southard, Beth Haas, Cammie McGovern, Peggy Orenstein, Steven Okazaki, Lisa Stewart, Scott Rudin, Eric Steel, Catherine Gottlieb, Ron Bernstein, the Portland crew, the Darien posse, and Alicia Gordon have all offered ongoing encouragement, support, insight, good food, and occasional lodging at crucial junctures throughout.

Dan Coyle, Joel Lovell, Miles Harvey, and Bill Lychack are four of the finest writers, editors, and friends I know and each read this book in various incarnations, taking time out of their busy schedule to bring a sharp eye to the text when most needed. To Bill, who talked me off several metaphorical ledges, I owe my prized Whiffle ball bat.

As well, I'd like to thank Nicholas Delbanco, Charlie Baxter, and Anton Shammas for showing me how.

Finally, it's hard to write a book without imagining a few people who might find what you write mildly interesting. To my family—my parents, Richard and Marianne, who read drafts of this book and helped fact-check and transcribe interviews; my brothers, Stephen, John, and Richard; my grandmother Rose; and Anne Marie Dowd, Kelly Grossi, and Michelle D'Ambrose; as well as the Corbett family, Chris, Matt, Steve, and Nanny—I have my most forgiving audience, without whom I'd be entirely lost. To my parents in particular, this humbled son says thank you, thank you.

My greatest friend, reader, and partner in crime is Sara Corbett. No single page slipped her detection. All of what's good belongs to her.

About the Author

Michael Paterniti's writing has appeared in publications including *The New York Times Magazine*, *National Geographic*, *Harper's*, *Outside*, *Esquire*, and *GQ*, where he works as a correspondent. He is the author of *Driving Mr. Albert*, *The Telling Room*, and *Love and Other Ways of Dying*. He lives in Portland, Maine, with his wife, the writer Sara Corbett, and their three children.

Twitter: @MikePaterniti

Printed in the United States
by Baker & Taylor Publisher Services